TROUT FISHING
IN
BEAUTIFUL
SOUTHERN
MONTANA

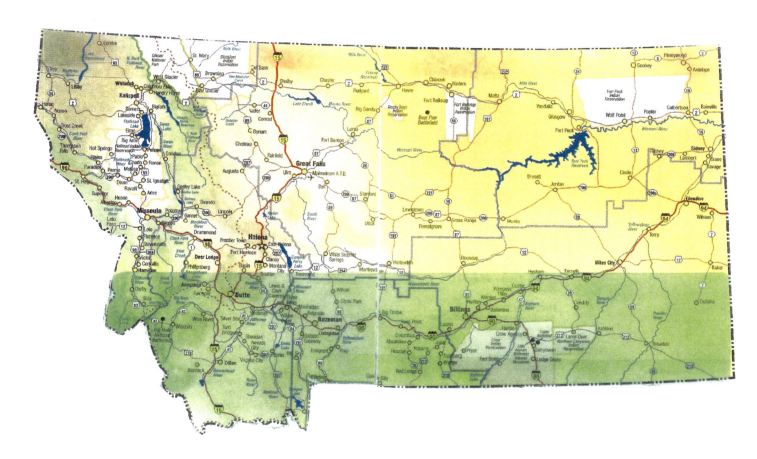

"Under the big sky of Montana, you'll discover some of the greatest natural and cultural treasures on earth. From stunning scenery and dazzling waters to geologic wonders and cultural history. Montana offers something for everyone. The diverse recreational and educational opportunities make this a great place to live and special place to visit."
Governor Switzer

THE COLORFUL

SPECIES

OF TROUT

IN SOUTHERN

MONTANA

AND THEIR
RELATIVES
IN THE
SALMONIDAE
FAMILY:
THE WHITEFISH
AND GRAYLING

WHERE THEY
ARE FOUND
IN MONTANA
IN PURPLE

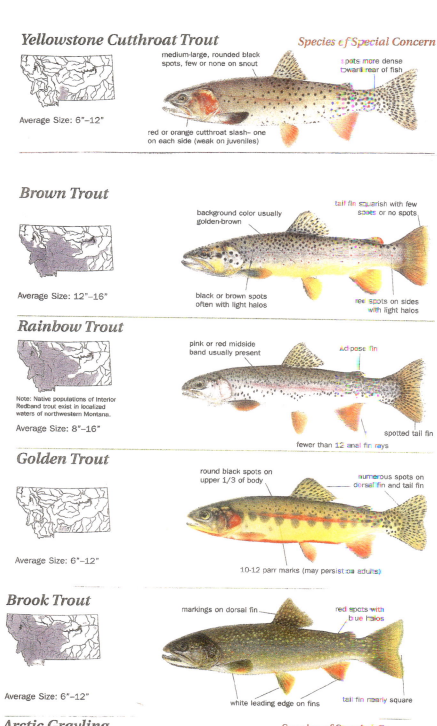

Yellowstone Cutthroat Trout

Species of Special Concern

Average Size: 6"–12"

medium-large, rounded black spots, few or none on snout

spots more dense toward rear of fish

red or orange cutthroat slash– one on each side (weak on juveniles)

Brown Trout

Average Size: 12"–16"

background color usually golden-brown

tail fin squarish with few spots or no spots

black or brown spots often with light halos

red spots on sides with light halos

Rainbow Trout

Note: Native populations of Interior Redband trout exist in localized waters of northwestern Montana.

Average Size: 8"–16"

pink or red midside band usually present

Adipose fin

spotted tail fin

fewer than 12 anal fin rays

Golden Trout

Average Size: 6"–12"

round black spots on upper 1/3 of body

numerous spots on dorsal fin and tail fin

10-12 parr marks (may persist on adults)

Brook Trout

Average Size: 6"–12"

markings on dorsal fin

red spots with blue halos

white leading edge on fins

tail fin nearly square

Arctic Grayling

Species of Special Concern

Average Size: 6"-12"

large scales

dorsal fin large, colorful, and sail-like

dark spots on front half of body

Mountain Whitefish

Average Size: 6"–12"

no spots on back

large scales

mouth small, no teeth

 Library of Congress

Shaw, Clayton
    Trout Fishing in Beautiful Southern Montana

ISBN   978-0692644683

TROUT FISHING IN BEAUTIFUL SOUTHERN MONTANA

AUTHOR: Clayton <u>Gene</u> Shaw

GRAPHIC ILLUSTRATIONS, PHOTO MANIPULATION, FORMATTING Autumn Frey

PHOTOGRAPHY Steve Rathburn, Ken Marsh, Merv Coleman

ACKNOWLEDGMENTS
> <u>Contributors:</u>
>> Montana Fish, Wildlife & Parks:
>>> Mike Ruggles, Fisheries Biologist, Billings
>>> Earl Radonski, Fisheries Tech III
>>
>> Steve Rathburn
>> Eric Beebe
>> Richard C. Romersa
>> Jim Harrison, Fly Fishing Guide
>> Other authorities
>
> <u>Research</u>
>> Monica Marsh
>
> <u>Cover Design</u>
>> Rosalie Shaw
>> Julie Shields
>
> **Proof Readers**
>> Monica Marsh
>> Peggy Walks

REFERENCES
> *Angler's Guide To Montana*   by Mike Sample
> *The Montanan's Fishing Guide*   by Dick Konizeski
> *Trout Fishing*   by Joe Brooks
> *Trout*   by Dick Sterberg
> *The Orvis Fly Fishing Guide*   by Tom Rosenbauer
> *Montana Sporting Journal*
> *Flies, The Best One Thousand*   by Randle Scott Stetzer
> Video *Successful Fly Fishing Strategies*   by Gary LaFontaine and Dick Sharon
> Video Sporting Fly vol 6   *Beaverhead River Montana*
> Video Sporting Fly vol 5   *Madison River Montana*
> *Trout* magazine by Trout Unlimited
> *2012 Annual Fishing Newsletter* by the MFW&P
> *2012 Montana Fishing Regulations*

TABLE OF CONTENTS

INTRODUCTION

SPECIAL THANKS

To the MONTANA FISH, WILDLIFE AND PARKS for the generous time they spent assisting with a more accurate understanding of the nature of trout and their habits. They shed light on their activities to maintain the trout fisheries and the trout population, with much attention given to the premier trout stream in the country, the Big Horn River The contributions of Mike Ruggles and Earl Rodonski were especially helpful, including a comprehensive list of the high mountain lakes in the Absaroka/Beartooth Wilderness.

SPECTACULAR BEARTOOTH MOUNTAINS
HELLROARING PLATEAU

SOUTHERN MOUNTANA
SNOW CAPPED MOUNTAINS   ROLLING GREEN HILLS

CRAZY MOUNTAINS

THESE PICTURESQUE MOUNTAINS JUST NORTHEAST OF LIVINGSTON, MONTANA, ARE THE ORIGIN OF NICE TROUT STREAMS WITH CONVENIENT CAMP GROUNDS. WHY ARE THEY CALLED THE "CRAZY" MOUNTAINS? THE STORY THAT'S BEEN HANDED DOWN IS THAT WHEN A PIONEER WAGON TRAIN WAS PASSING THROUGH MONTANA, A WOMAN LEFT THE TRAIN AND GOT LOST IN THESE MOUNTAINS. WHEN THEY FOUND HER, SHE WAS CRAZY. DOES THAT SEEM LOGICAL? WHY ELSE WOULD THEY BE CALLED SUCH?

INTRODUCTION

The majority of Americans live in what you might say is a "concrete/asphalt jungle". They live much of their lives with the constant buzz of traffic, honking of horns, revving of engines and all the other noises associated with the city. Why not get away from it all for a nice quiet refreshing vacation? We heartily recommend beautiful southern Montana. It is an excellent place for families from out of state to visit, take in the sights, and enjoy many outdoor activities. One of the main reasons many come to the area is for the outstanding trout fishing which is gaining in popularity.

There are numerous guest ranches and lodges with excellent rooming and dining outfitters ready to take you on horseback into high mountains to sightsee or fish. There are guides to take you boating, white water rafting, or trout fishing on beautiful streams and crystal clear lakes. There are many back roads that can take you to some breathtaking scenery.

Montana has been called the "big sky country" and anyone who has visited the state can see why- perhaps because it is an agricultural state with less pollution. Compared to most states the air is clear, prompting one visitor from New York to say jokingly, "I don't know if I can trust air I can't see". Southern Montana not only has the big sky but some of the most majestic mountain ranges in America, rising over 10,000 feet, hosting hundreds of lakes above timberline. Sprinkle in some breathtaking cascades and waterfalls. Out of these mountains flow some blue ribbon trout streams, most noteworthy of which is the longest free flowing river in the United States, the Yellowstone River.

One main attraction is trout fishing in southern Montana, a trout fisherman's paradise. We recommend you try the sport, especially with imitation flies. It is a skill that is acquired over time, and has become an addiction to many. To be on a mountain stream on a warm August morning where the sun glistens off the crystal clear water, casting your line into some nice looking fishing holes, and anticipating a strike by a hungry trout, is exciting to say the least. Landing a colorful mountain trout in the warm sun and cool mountain air is an thrilling experience.

I have fished in Minnesota for bass and pike, in Idaho for steelhead, and in the ocean for various fish, but in my opinion nothing compares to the fun and challenge of trout fishing on a mountain stream. Trout are a beautiful creature with very artistic coloring which is a testimony to the artistic ability of the Creator. The Rocky Mountain range along the Wyoming border produces the beautiful streams that will be discussed and also hundreds of high mountain lakes, home to several species of trout including the golden trout.

Backpackers hike into these areas and stay for days fishing in numerous lakes, a short distance from one another.

There are several ways to catch trout such as using bait and spin fishing with metal lures, but the most exciting for many fishermen is using imitation flies, especially dry flies. Some anglers fish only with flies and are referred to as "purists". This form of trout fishing is the most challenging because it requires more extensive knowledge of the traits of trout, especially their feeding habits and hangouts in the water. Also, one needs to know the techniques of how to cast and work the fly on the water. One can only become really skilled after years of doing it. In fact, it is a never ending learning experience. Much of the discussion in this book relates to stream fishing because that is the most challenging and, in my opinion, the most enjoyable.

One objective of this book is to provide insight into trout fishing drawing on my years of experience, various books and contributions from other skilled men or women. Hopefully, it will provide the right help for someone wanting to become a skilled angler. The book is intended to provide with as much simplicity as possible a description of how and where to catch trout in southern Montana. Thorough research has been done and many veteran fishermen interviewed to get a consensus of what truly is effective. The objective is to produce a narrative that is broad, reliable and accurate. This book is designed to get one started, and help him or her find success at it in a relatively short time. A warning, however, as was said, it is addictive!

Trout fishing is not for everyone, but many who try it get to love it. I was about five years old when my grandfather began taking me on fishing trips to the Stillwater river near where we lived. At about six years of age I caught my first trout, around 10 inches long. At that point it became a favorite pastime, and I could not get enough of it. Later my parents began taking me fishing which became an every-weekend affair during spring, summer and fall. It goes without saying I learned a great deal about trout fishing from a very early age. I have read books on the subject but nothing takes the place of actually doing it. Nonetheless, it usually does not take long for a novice to start catching some fish. I have personally assisted some people who became quite successful at it rather quickly.

There are several species of trout and all have their own habits. Besides this, there are many other factors involved that one needs to learn. To successfully bring home a catch or go home "skunked", which means to not catch any, depends to a large part on how well one understands these factors.. However, it does not take long to start catching fish, and even if you do not catch any, the fun is still there. It helps a great deal if you are patient as there are times when fishing can be poor for no apparent reason.

Whereas I enjoy stream fishing the best, many like to fish the lakes or even hike into high mountain areas where fish are easy to catch. Some of these lakes contain the golden trout which has fabulous colors, especially when it is first pulled out of the water. These trout are worth the trip which usually entails a difficult climb. In most cases they exist in lakes above 7000 feet.

Along the Montana-Wyoming border are the beautiful Beartooth mountains. One particular stretch directly west of Rock Creek drainage above timberline are the Hell Roaring and Silver Run Plateaus, littered with good trout fishing lakes. Due west for about 30 miles from these plateaus are hundreds of high mountain lakes, some containing large trout.

Overall, I prefer to fish in a somewhat large mountain stream that has some fair sized brown or rainbow trout. I personally find this to be the most challenging and exciting. Fly fishing in particular has become the preference of a big share of men and more recently women. All I can say is "try it, you'll like it."

The purpose of this book is not only to provide the information necessary to take up trout fishing but also to help anglers, including their families, to vacation in southern Montana and know where to go and find lodging. Many of the lodges and guest ranches have a variety of entertaining things to do for both adults and children. In some cases only some of the family fish while the others want some other type of recreation, such as sightseeing. To address this, the book has sections that detail different excursions that families may take other than fishing. The state has a lot to offer in the way of outdoor and other cultural activity. In summary the objective is to provide the whole gamut of information for families to have a good time.

CHAPTER 1

THE TROUT STREAMS

SOUTHERN MONTANA TROUT STREAMS

There are numerous trout streams in southern Montana all of them coming out of the mountain ranges to the south by the Wyoming border and west by the Idaho border. Most of them flow out of the snow capped Beartooth/Absaroka mountain range and northward through some beautiful valleys and canyons.

The streams that we will consider are the following going from east to west: Big Horn, Clark's Fork, Rock Creek, Stillwater, Rosebud, Boulder, Yellowstone, Musselshell, Gallatin, Madison, Ruby, Beaverhead, Red Rock, and Big Hole River. There are other streams in the south, but these are the main ones that we will consider.   These streams are readily accessible by road and offer excellent trout fishing. Also, they all have tributaries flowing into them that have, in most cases, pan size trout. We will discuss the attributes of each of the main streams starting with the Big Horn.

Before going to fish any Montana stream, it is necessary to check the Montana Fish Wildlife and Parks (MFW&P) regulations covering it. You should know such things as the limit in possession, is it catch and release, and other requirements which can be found in the publication *Montana Fishing Regulations* made available when getting a fishing license. We have not included maps of the streams because it would be more helpful to have a copy of the *Montana Atlas and Gazetteer* which contains detailed topographical maps of all areas of the state. It shows where all the campgrounds and fishing accesses are located for every stream in the state. In the front it lists all the main fisheries in the state and the species of trout in each one.

People ask about stocking streams. According to the MFW&P this is no longer done. It became evident that this practice was actually counterproductive to the population growth of trout. There is one exception; the cutthroat trout is being brought back in many areas. For various reasons it had greatly diminished in numbers.

Overall, it is best to go to an area on a stream that is not heavily fished. You can do this by going to a rancher or farmer and ask permission to fish on his land. Most of the time they will consent. If he consents, be sure to show respect for his property by not leaving gates open or committing other careless actions. According to Montana law, you can fish anywhere on any stream as long as you are below the high water line. There are land owners who are challenging this law. Also, there are special restrictions when on an Indian reservation.

BIG HORN RIVER
FLOAT IT OR WADE IT

BIG HORN RIVER

The Big Horn river, which flows out of yellowtail dam and through the Crow Indian reservation, has become a very popular blue ribbon trout stream in the U.S. due to the fact the trout are large and plentiful. Some say it is the best trout stream in the country. Due to the fact that it goes through the reservation special regulations apply. Currently, live bait can be used the first 600 feet below the dam, however, the regulations for this river change more frequently. It is best to check what the current MFW&P *Montana Fishing Regulations* booklet has to say.

Food in the river is abundant and the water temperature is moderated by the dam and as such it is called a tailwater. This helps the fish to grow rapidly.

Many fishermen like to float the river and fish from a raft or boat, setting in at the dam and floating 13 miles to an access. Others will float and stop at some spot and wade, fish, or walk downstream from the dam. In the spring the rainbows are spawning and moving up stream which enhances the fishing. Actually, it can be fished year round as the river does not freeze over. As to what flies work the best on the Big Horn, the main ones are listed in the chapter *Popular Tied Flies.*

YELLOWSTONE RIVER

This beautiful river is the longest free-flowing river in North America. It has not been dammed up at any point. Yellowstone lake in Yellowstone park is where it originates. The lake and the river at its headwaters contains the very desirable cutthroat trout, reportedly the oldest native trout of Montana. For a time the lake became contaminated with lake trout which feed on cutthroat minnows and caused a significant drop in the cutthroat population. Currently there is a strong effort to destroy the lake trout population and bring the cutthroat back.

The river has a very majestic and colorful waterfall, the Yellowstone Falls, which is actually in Yellowstone park in Wyoming. The waters above the falls are inhabited by Cutthroat, whereas below the falls to the north into Montana are the brown and rainbow trout. Coming into Montana the river goes through a fairly rugged canyon and then widens out into a beautiful green valley.

Upstream from the small town of Columbus this excellent trout river has been a popular attraction for some well known trout fishermen such as Joe Brooks and Ted Trueblood, popular authors on trout fishing. It has been rated a blue ribbon trout stream by the experts.

When the water is high but clear it is a good time to fish with spinners. The river gets quite wide in some places but being equipped with a quality open-bail spinning real and a five or six foot rod, one can reach pools by the opposite bank. These pools are not fished as often and produce more strikes.

It is a favorite fly fishing river in the early spring and fall but is too high and murky during the late spring and summer runoff.. Due to its size there are more large fish caught than in the smaller streams. The brown and rainbow trout have very distinct habits and veteran fishermen make use of the difference as to how they fish for them. (See the chapter 5)

From the town of Gardiner near Yellowstone Park to the town of Livingston on Interstate 90 the river flows south through a canyon called Paradise Valley with numerous fishing accesses and a very popular resort, Chico Hot Springs. The resort has excellent lodging, many recreational activities for families and is a favorite of Billings residents. From this location one can readily do trout fishing or travel through Yellowstone Park either to sightsee or fish for some very nice cutthroat trout.

Another fish, related to the trout family, is the whitefish that some go after in the Yellowstone in the Winter. It is sometimes referred to as the "Montana bone fish" because when eating them it is difficult to separate the small bones from the meat, unlike the trout. Some fish for them mainly because they are good to eat smoked. In the winter there is a midge called the snow fly, and fishermen have some success fishing for the whitefish using an imitation of it. These winter fishermen, going after whitefish, typically use long bamboo poles that reach out over the ice sometimes with maggots for bait.

The Yellowstone is a popular river to float when the water is not too high. Of course, the advantage of floating is you get to fish a great variety of water that is not fished so often. Some stop at various places where there are nice holes and even camp overnight. There are nice float trips in both directions from Billings that provide good fishing, and there are guides available for them. To the west there are designated trips all along for over 100 miles from Billings clear to Gardiner near Yellowstone Park. East from Billings fishermen catch many other kinds of fish including bass.

In August many anglers from out of state come to the National Trout Derby in the vicinity of Livingston, a small town located where the river comes out of the mountains. At times there have been a thousand or more participating, and those catching the biggest fish receive prizes.

THE MIGHTY YELLOWSTONE RIVER
AT IT'S SOURCE - YELLOWSTONE PARK

YELLOWSTONE RIVER   by Livingston

CLARKS FORK

This somewhat small river flows out of Wyoming all the way from the mountains at the northeast corner of Yellowstone Park and eventually into the Yellowstone river about 15 miles west of Billings. In the headwaters and above the town of Bridger there is good fishing for brook trout, which are not as common in the state as the brown and rainbow trout.

The upper waters make for good fly fishing. Brook trout are found more in the upper waters by the boarder and into Wyoming. Except for the upper sections in the mountains, like the Big Horn, it is not a particularly scenic river by comparison to the streams to the west.

If one is looking for some good brook trout fishing and plans to spend more than a day, a suggested place to lodge is Cook City near the northeast entrance to Yellowstone Park. This is a small mountain town that has motels and cabins for lodging and some small ma-and-pa cafes with good food. In this area the stream crisscrosses the Montana/Wyoming border as it flows east from Cook City. It eventually exits the mountains and runs through farm land heading north. Fishing in this area will require either a Montana or Wyoming fishing license, depending on exactly where you are.

ROCK CREEK

This creek runs through the popular ski resort, Red Lodge, about 60 miles southwest of Billings. The headwaters are near the famous Beartooth Pass which reaches over 11,000 feet high on the Wyoming border. Above Red Lodge it is a very picturesque stream flowing through a beautiful canyon with numerous camp grounds.

It is a fun stream to fish with dry flies. During the busy tourist season, June to August, it is necessary to reserve, well in advance, campground space if you want to fish Rock Creek above Red Lodge in the mountains. Some families rent a motel room in Red Lodge, and fish the stream right where it runs through town, taking advantage of the picnic facilities   Often, rainbow trout can be caught there. A campground about 10 miles above Red Lodge is near a small lake that is well stocked with small rainbow trout, and ideally suited for children to fish. Red Lodge is a quaint little town with numerous western shops to accommodate the hundreds of tourists.

ROCK CREEK
A SMALL STREAM WITH RAINBOWS

STILLWATER
RIVER
HEAD WATERS

STILLWATER RIVER   WEST OF ABSAROKEE

STILLWATER RIVER

I was born in the small southern town of Columbus which is near my favorite trout stream, the Stillwater river. At the age of five I began going with my grandfather and uncle to fish it and continued, somewhat on and off, over the next 50 years. I prefer to fish this river over all the others with the exception of the Madison. It has a beautiful uniqueness to it. It meanders down through one of the most gorgeous canyons you will find anywhere. This canyon, towards the upper part of the river, contains scenic high-rising bluffs on both sides and in the river are large boulders which make for good fishing holes. The name of this river does not accurately describe its features - it has plenty of fast water.

If one so desires, you can follow the river on paved road up into the mountains passing a high-mountain waterfall on the way to Woodbine campground. Just a hundred yards beyond you come to the Woodbine canyon where a cascade roars through the canyon making for breath-taking scenery. Above this canyon is a small scenic lake, home to the colorful brock trout.
.

A favorite site to fish is the Castlerock campground which lies about 15 miles west of the small town of Absarokee.. This stretch of river has a beautiful fishing hole that extends about a hundred yards. Most fishermen who come to this spot spend much of their time fishing this hole. I, however, like to fish the stretch of water just below the hole. What most inexperienced trout fishermen do not notice is that this stretch of water has a sandbar running down the middle of it. Along the opposite bank is deeper water inhabited by some nice browns. After the spring runoff and when the water has receded, you can wade out to the sandbar and cast flies to it and snag some beauties. It makes for easy casting because you do not have the heavy brush at your back. Many times I have caught several fish within two hours. Keep in mind, however, that this characteristic of the river exists now, but it may not exist in the future. River beds change over the course of time.

STILLWATER RIVER

NEAR WOODBINE

CASTLEROCK

EAST ROSEBUD SCENIC MOUNTAIN RIVER
TRIBUTARY OF THE STILLWATER

The Stillwater valley has been the home to several sheep ranches, some of which have disappeared because of being subdivided for cabins along the water. One can still see herds of sheep grazing on the hillsides and at times see sheepherder wagons here and there. In the areas above Castlerock campground, the valley becomes wide open country with much less brush along the river. This makes for nice fly fishing because you do not have the hazard of brush directly behind you.

About five miles above Castlerock, the west fork enters the main stream. At this location is the small community of Nye, just a wide spot in the road. The west fork is much smaller but is a good producer of pan-size brown trout. There are some campgrounds on the west fork and the scenery is beautiful.

Further up the main Stillwater is the Stillwater mine that produces two precious elements, platinum and paladium. On top of the mine's mountain one can see the West fork below and also one of the most beautiful flowered meadows. A good place to rest and feast your eyes!

A few miles further up the river is the Woodbine campground. It has the trailhead from which one can hike 33 miles along the upper Stillwater all the way to a summit called Daisy Pass, a short distance from Cook City near the entrance to Yellowstone Park. To make this hike trip one needs to plan at least four days, preferably five, so you are not rushed. It is best to start the hike at the south end, at Daisy Pass, because it is downhill from there. Along the way you come to Souix Charlie lake near Woodbine and home to small, but eatable, brook trout. The lower part of this campground has a trail that leads up the mountain to a two-part waterfall. The scenery there is well worth the hike.

A stream that runs into the Stillwater, and also has very good fishing, is the Rosebud river. At the headwaters of the west fork of this river are two beautiful lakes, Emerald and West Rosebud. Near here a trail starts that begins a steady climb for three miles to the Mystic Dam. From here the trail continues a long hike up to more lakes, one of which is Silver lake. This lake has a silvery bottom which allows you to easily see the trout in it. You have no doubt as to where to throw your line.

The East fork of the Rosebud leads to East Rosebud lake. From here one can hike all the way to Cook City. However, this hike entails extensive climbing to the top of a plateau where there are many more lakes. Fossil lake is at the top and has some excellent fishing. If you get there at the right time you can catch beautiful 14 to 16 inch rainbows. From Fossil Lake it is about a eight mile hike downhill to a camp site on highway 212 near Cook City.

↑

FLOWS INTO
BOTTOM HERE

BOULDER RIVER
NATURAL BRIDGE

FLOWS OUT
HERE →

NATURAL BRIDGE FALLS
LOOKING DOWNSTREAM FROM THE TOP OF THE FALLS

BOULDER RIVER ABOVE NATURAL BRIDGE FALLS

BOULDER RIVER

This stream is somewhat smaller than the Stillwater, but it has a lot of the same characteristics. The majority of the fish are brown trout but occasionally one will bring in a nice rainbow. The river lives up to its name because it contains a lot of large boulders. This makes for nice fishing because boulders cause whirling pools of water behind them in which the trout like to hang out. In a sense, it gives you an idea of where they are. In the upper Boulder where the river runs between high mountains, there are very large boulders in it. It is a very picturesque place with some good fishing.

This river, like the Stillwater, is in a very majestic mountainous setting. It has an unusual but beautiful waterfall called Natural Bridge Falls located about 40 miles south of Big Timber, a small town on the east-west interstate 90 highway. It is called this because the river drops through a hole in the rock bottom and shoots out the side of a rock cavern, forming a roaring waterfall into a large swirling pool below. This is a very picturesque part of the river that is a scenic photographer's dream. The author has tried to capture the full beauty of it on film, but no picture seems to quite do it justice.

There are numerous fishing accesses and campgrounds where you can go. Thirty miles south of Big Timber there is a small community called McCloud where the river west fork enters the main fork. On the west fork there are not too many open places to fish. However, if you ask a rancher about fishing on his land he will normally allow it. They appreciate it when you ask. This fork of the stream is not fished very heavily and thus one can usually come home with a pretty good catch of brown trout.

You can drive into the mountains on the main fork until you get to a trail head, from which ambitious backpackers climb to Lake Plateau above timberline. There are numerous lakes in fairly close proximity making for good fishing and camping.

MUSSLESHELL RIVER

This relatively small stream runs east and west about 50 miles north of Billings. It has mostly fair sized brown trout, and has good fly fishing at certain times of the year. For those living or lodging in Billings, it is just a short drive to some excellent stretches of water.

GALLATIN RIVER   IN SCENIC GALLATIN CANYON

31

GALLATIN RIVER

GALLATIN RIVER
HEAD WATER
ABOVE 6000 FT

MAJESTIC
ROCKY
MOUNTAINS

Our family has at numerous times stayed in a place called Solberg's Cabins that rents units (without bedding) that sit right on the stream. We have caught several fish around two pounds. (See the pictures in the appendix).

GALLATIN RIVER

The headwaters of this river is in the mountains just west of Yellowstone Park. The well paved highway 191 follows it into the mountains all the way south from interstate 90 just west of Bozeman. There are numerous fishing accesses along the way. It is a beautiful river that descends rapidly in some areas of the Gallatin canyon, a popular attraction for kayaks and float trips.

After coming out of the mountains it flows through the somewhat famous Gallatin valley where Bozeman, on interstate 90, is located. This valley is known for its rich soil and fabulous green meadows that contains numerous small spring creeks with trout. As a boy I fished these creeks many times, just walking distance from Bozeman and came home with a creel full of nice browns using a simple barbed hook with a worm. While attending college, I and a school mate fished the Gallatin in the valley area, sometimes in early morning before classes. We never went home empty handed.

As with other streams under discussion the Gallatin has beautiful scenery and a wide variety of water flow, in some areas nothing but white water for hundreds of yards. While the predominant fish is the brown, one can occasionally snag a brook, rainbow or cutthroat. It is an ideal stream for fly fishing, in particular dry flies. Even though the city of Bozeman is near and would seem to contribute to excessive fishing it really has not become "fished out."

Most of the river in the Gallatin canyon has a good variety of fast and slow water. The fishing is good but the best fly fishing water is in the area just south of Big Sky Resort, about 30 miles south of Bozeman. The river widens out in several places which lends itself to wading out into the stream and fishing in both directions. I especially like this type of water for flies, especially dry flies. At the upper waters the river meanders for miles through a beautiful meadow which attracts a lot of fishermen. It is easy to fish as there is very little brush along the banks.

Bozeman is an interesting city in that it seems to be a haven for sports minded people; fishermen, hunters, backpackers, snowmobilers, and skiers. As a result land values have skyrocketed, although this has been moderated by the recession of 2008.

If an out-of-state angler for trout visits the area, there are excellent tackle shops that can provide the latest in trout fishing gear and information on the what and where of current fishing

All in all, the Gallatin area is a beautiful and interesting place in which many from other states have come to procure a second home. If the reader plans to check into this, be sure to bring lots of money.

MADISON RIVER

This river was at one time described by professional fly fishermen as the premier trout stream in the United States. It is still in my opinion about the most enjoyable stream to fish. There has been strong legal effort to keep it this way and therefore it is, at the time of this writing, strictly catch and release for most of the river above Ennis lake. It does without doubt have some excellent characteristics that make for good fly fishing. There are long sections where it winds through meadows in a broad valley with very little brush thus making it easy to cast without getting your line tangled. The stream produces fairly large fish and maintains a large population, over 3000 fish/mile, due to the catch and release regulation and extensive food in the water.

There are two distinct areas of the Madison: the upper Madison which is the river above Ennis lake in a broad valley between two mountain ranges, and the lower part below the lake which is in hills and prairie country. The features of each are distinctly different The waters in the lower part, below beartrap canyon, tend to have excessive moss in summer and fall, but are conduce to trout growth. The upper part tends to be spread out with clear water, rocky bottom, and other features more desirable for fly fishing.

The lower Madison leaves Ennis lake and flows into the Beartrap canyon where it descends quickly making for fast water, while further downstream it eventually flows slowly through more open area.   It is rumored that this area is home to some of the largest populations of rattle snakes in the country. The little town of Norris, nearby, at one time had a shop where you could buy all kinds of rattlesnake items. The store had at one time a skin of a very large specimen that went almost from ceiling to floor.

In the mid 1900s the lower Madison was inhabited by very large browns and rainbows, some in excess of ten pounds. Part of the reason for the extra ordinarily large fish is because of the abundant food in the water, including crawfish. Today there are still very large ones but not as plentiful. One time we fished the river during the salmon fly hatch. We were sleeping in our camper when the hatch arrived. (The salmon fly hatch starts in the lower part of a river where there is warmer water and slowly progresses upstream) From our camper I heard what sounded like someone throwing boulders into the water. Large trout were in a feeding frenzy and sometimes jumping several feet into the air to grab an airborne salmon fly. This exciting event will only last for a few days in any one area. We grabbed our poles and almost immediately were pulling in fish in excess of five pounds. One fisherman nearby hooked a very large trout, possibly ten pounds, on a fly rod and was trying to reel it in with much difficulty. I went to help net the fish, but the line broke. Out of anger he threw his rod and reel into the middle of the river and stormed off. I might have been tempted to do the same.
In late summer and fall the abundant moss in the river makes it difficult to fish with lures. The best bet is to fish with dry flies and maintain them on the surface to avoid the moss.

MADISON RIVER South of Ennis

Wide open access - excellent fly fishing

The upper Madison, as was mentioned, is more like fishing in the mountains. For this reason, I prefer the upper part because it is wide open and a fairly large river, ideal for fly fishing. You might say it is fly fisherman friendly. To add to that, the scenery is breathtaking, having snow capped mountains on both sides.

The river flows through the small town of Ennis with fishing accesses nearby. The trout are predominantly browns and rainbows. There is also a sizeable population of whitefish which is an indication of the health of the river. Whitefish do not do well in polluted water.

Twenty five miles west of Ennis is the town of Virginia City, an old restored gold and ruby mining town. Families can combine some nice site seeing to go with their fishing.

The Madison flows out of Hebgen Lake near Yellowstone Park and then into nearby Quake Lake. This lake is a result of an 1959 earthquake induced mountain slide that dropped onto the lake and dammed it up. From there it rapidly descends west into Madison Valley. Hebgen lake, near the epicenter, had its north shore drop several feet due to the quake (note the picture of the cabin in the water). At the site of the slide there is a interesting memorial describing the event.

RUBY RIVER
The Ruby River has browns and cutthroat trout, but it does not draw the anglers like the nearby premier streams such as the Madison. It has a lot of private land and owners are not very accommodating to fishermen inquiring to fish on their land. However, if one were to get permission to fish on some private land, it could prove to be very good.

BEAVERHEAD RIVER
Some say this river competes with the Big Horn river to the west as the premier trout stream in Montana. It flows out of a dam as does the Big Horn. It produces big fish for the same reason that the Big Horn River does, namely, the water is warmer due to the dam, and it has an abundance of food in the water. For the most part it is a slow meandering stream with heavy brush along its banks, which makes it difficult to wade fish. For this reason, it is a favorite stream to float and fish. The predominant trout are browns and rainbows.

BIG HOLE RIVER
Considered a very scenic river in some areas, this river starts at the Idaho boarder in the Beaverhead mountains and cycles through southwestern Montana for 155 miles. At its source it is surrounded by towering mountains, and where it exits the mountains it enters the Big Hole River Valley. This breathtaking valley, at more than 6000 feet elevation, has the Pioneer Mountains to the east and the Beaverhead Mountains to the west. The predominant fish in this

section, the headwaters in the mountains down to the community of Wise River, are the brook trout and grayling.

The valley is somewhat desolate. The largest town is Wisdom and there is not much in the way of services. It flows for 60 miles in Big Hole Valley, after which, it enters a canyon and descends more rapidly for 30 miles and eventually combines with the Beaverhead and Ruby Rivers to form the Jefferson River. The predominant trout below Wise River are the rainbow and brown trout, both of which are quite abundant, reportedly about 2,500 fish/mile at the time of this writing..

As it flows through the Big Hole River Valley, it is fed by numerous streams coming out of the pioneer mountains, many of which provide good trout fishing. The whole area of the valley and surrounding mountains offers excellent scenery along with the good fishing. A tributary, Big Lake Creek, has the Twin Lakes at its headwaters and a campground. Miner Creek also has a campground well into the mountains.

In the fall the Big Hole River Valley is very colorful due to many cottonwoods with their beautiful yellow leaves. At this time it is good fishing for brooks and browns that are spawning.

RED ROCK RIVER
This river in the upper stretches does provide some excellent fly fishing for cutthroats and grayling. It flows into the two Red Rock lakes where fishing is prohibited, including the connecting stream and immediate surrounding areas. The restriction is due to the fact that it is a designated wildlife refuge and breeding ground for the trumpeter swan, which came close to extinction, has since been highly protected and kept undisturbed. The area is surrounded by country that has some good trout fishing streams, but fishermen must stay away from the refuge.

The river flows out of lower Red Rock Lake and flows through Centennial Valley and into the Lima Reservoir. This beautiful valley is home to a great variety of birds and is also blanketed with flowers. After the reservoir the fishing is nothing exceptional, and much of this stretch is private land. The river intersects Interstate 15 and follows it north to Clark Canyon Reservoir which is a popular recreational spot with good fishing for brown and rainbow trout.

CHAPTER 2
SOUTHERN MONTANA LAKES

There are a number of lakes that are accessible by road with excellent campground facilities. The most common type of fishing is trolling by boat Others prefer to still fish from shore using a bobber and bait, usually nightcrawler worms. It can be most relaxing, just sitting in your folding chair watching your bobber, and enjoying good conversation with your companion. The high mountain lakes are good for just about any type of bait, fly, or spin fishing.

Many like to backpack into high lakes of the Beartooth/Absaroka Mountain range, where there is a variety in the type and size of trout available. The main ones are the rainbow, cutthroat, brook and golden trout. In addition, you can get helpful information on these lakes from the book, *"The Montanan's Fishing Guide"* by Konizeski which will steer you to the best high lakes and away from the ones too difficult to reach.

The following lakes are accessible by road, or are the main ones that can be hiked into on a well defined trail. For a more complete list of the high mountain lakes, see the chapter *High Mountain Lakes*.

BIG HORN LAKE

This is a very large reservoir behind the Yellowtail Dam in southeastern Montana on the Crow Indian reservation. Flowing from it is the Big Horn river, home to very large brown trout. The lake stretches for over 30 miles partly into Wyoming. It is an enjoyable place to take a family with small children.

The best way to fish it is by boat with an outboard motor or with a large pontoon platform boat with an enclosure for overnight sleeping. The latter is nice for families because they can fish, or swim or hang close to shore and do a little hiking. The type of terrain is mostly prairie country with lots of wildlife, especially deer.

The lake is in a deep canyon, and the water contains not just trout, but many of the fish found in midwestern lakes such as bass and pike. The main attraction is not so much fishing, but other water activities such as boating..

LAKES OF THE HELL ROARING AND SILVER RUN PLATEAUS

Highway 212, southwest of Billings, runs along Rock Creek going through Red Lodge and into the Absaroka-Beartooth mountain range. This drive is one of the most scenic in North America, involving switchbacks up to the beautiful famous Beartooth Pass, which is on the Montana-Wyoming border, and reaches an elevation over 12,000 feet.

On the other side of Rock Creek drainage, is the Hell Roaring and Silver Run Plateaus, accessible only by a narrow dirt road. These plateaus and other plateaus of the Absaroka-Beartooth range to the west, contain several hundred lakes, all over 10,000 feet. From the end of the road, all of the lakes must be reached by foot. There are too many lakes to mention, but one, for example Moon lake, reportedly produces trout over five pounds. For good fishing, it is best to arrive just after the ice thaws. Backpackers usually camp within walking distance of several lakes. These high mountain plateaus are part of a range above timberline that goes for over 30 miles west from the Rock Creek drainage.

EAST ROSEBUD LAKE, RIMROCK LAKE, LAKE-AT-THE-FALLS, AND RAINBOW LAKE

These lakes are located about 75 miles southwest of Billings in the East Rosebud drainage of the Absaroka-Beartooth range. The first one is the very picturesque East Rosebud lake that can be reached by mountain road. Much of the land on the northern side of the lake, where the road is, is private which limits the fishing from shore. However, a trail head is close, from which one can reach the upper part of the lake and fish there. Backpackers can hike 30 miles from here all the way over a high mountain range to Cook City by Yellowstone Park. There are numerous lakes along the way including those listed above.

HEBGEN LAKE
"A LONG TIME AGO SOMEONE WAS NOT HAVING A GOOD DAY"

One can fish at the upper end of East Rosebud Lake or in the stream flowing into it. Backpackers usually prefer to fish the lakes above. However, it is a pretty good climb to get to them. The scenery is breathtaking and the fishing is excellent. These upper lakes are home to fair sized rainbows, brooks, cutthroat and the, somewhat rare, golden trout. Beyond these lakes, the trail is a difficult climb; but on top of the range there are other numerous lakes, one of which is Fossil Lake that has rainbows over two pounds. If you climb to the lakes at the top, above timberline, before June or after August 15, they may be frozen over. The best fishing is right after the thaw.

These lakes can be fished with flies, live bait, or spinners. When I fished them, I would use whatever worked the best, although I preferred flies.

SYLVAN LAKE AND CROW LAKE

These two lakes are in the mountains directly above East Rosebud Lake. A trailhead to reach them starts at East Rosebud Lake. The hike is a difficult one but many feel it is worth the effort. Some very nice golden trout, around 13 inches, are in Sylvan, and brook trout are in Crow Lake.

EMERALD, WEST ROSEBUD, MYSTIC, ISLAND, AND SILVER LAKE

These lakes are in the West Rosebud drainage southwest of Billings. It takes about an hour over graveled road to get to the first lake. I fished the Emerald Lake often when I was a young man, and in those days, large brown trout were plentiful there. The most common way to fish the lake was with spinners, especially hammered brass or silver daredevils. It was not uncommon to catch more than twenty trout in excess of two pounds. The lake is relatively shallow, and the trout could easily be seen in the water. It is a beautiful emerald colored lake, but somewhat shallow. In recent years, the fishing has diminished significantly.

The road continues past Emerald for about a mile to West Rosebud Lake, which is deeper and has plenty of rainbow trout. A good way to fish it is by boat, but I prefer still fishing from shore using a bobber and worm or grasshopper, if available. The rainbows are usually pan size, about ten inches.

COONEY DAM

This relatively small lake is just off Highway 212 south of Laurel, a small town 10 miles west of Billings. It has a good supply of rainbow trout that can get up to two pounds or better. It is not very scenic and there are few trees, so, when the temperature is high in June and July it can be unpleasant. Aside from this, it is a good place to take a family. It is a favorite place to ice fish during winter but in recent years the weather in Montana has been too warm for ice to build up enough.

LAKE ELMO

This small lake is in the Billings city limits at the northeast edge of town. It is stocked primarily with rainbow trout, but there is a variety of other fish including bass. It has a section with a nice beach for families with small children. Besides at this beach, swimming is allowed in all areas.

SIOUX CHARLEY LAKE

This small, but very picturesque lake, is located well into the mountains at the headwaters of the Stillwater River. To get to it from the road requires a hike of about a mile. It contains small brook trout in abundance.

MARTINSDALE LAKE and DEAD MAN'S BASIN

Approximately 100 miles northwest of Billings these two nice lakes sit in wide open prairie They have mostly brown trout that can get up to several pounds. Nearby is a small stream called the Musselshell, which also contains brown trout. On this stream my family and I have had reunions at a place called Solberg's Cabins, where small cabins, right on the stream, can be rented without bedding for a modest fee. The lakes are a short distance away.

ENNIS LAKE

About a 50 mile drive, west from Bozeman, sits Ennis Lake on the Madison River. This is a large lake that has brown, rainbow trout and an uncommon trout relative, the arctic grayling. My experience at this lake has been entirely still fishing from shore using live bait. Over the years, we caught several large browns and an occasional rainbow. It is in a beautiful setting, Madison Valley.

HEBGEN LAKE

Hebgen Lake sits adjacent to Yellowstone Park in the southwest corner of the state. The Madison River flows in and out of it. It contains browns, rainbows and cutthroat trout. Most of the fishing is done by boat and trolling, but one can access the lake at several places, and fish from shore using spinners or still fish using live bait.

QUAKE LAKE

This lake was formed by the earthquake of 1959, and sits on the Madison River just a few miles below Hebgen Lake. It has an eerie appearance due to the dead trees in the water. The lake contains brown and rainbow trout, and is generally fished by boat.

CLIFF LAKE AND WADE LAKE

Highway 287 follows the Madison River from Hebgen Lake going north. A few miles south of Quake Lake is a turn off that goes into the Beaverhead mountains, and ends up at these two lakes, where there are some nice campgrounds. These are very scenic lakes with some good fishing that is done primarily by boat. The fish are mostly browns and rainbows, but Cliff Lake has some cutthroat

CLARK CANYON RESERVOIR

This lake is a popular recreational area that has good fishing for brown and rainbow trout. It is located on Interstate 15 about 30 miles south of Dillon.

1959 EARTHQUAKE NEAR YELLOWSTONE PARK
Quake Lake formed by huge mountain slide into the Madison River
Some cabins on Hebgan lake ended up in the lake

HIGH MOUNTAIN LAKES, ROAD ACCESSIBLE
NEAR BEARTOOTH PASS, MONT/WYO BORDER

TWIN LAKES

In this photo you are looking down on two lakes, like emeralds in a beautiful mountain setting. They are the first lakes you see when you get near the top of Beartooth Pass. In the background, under cloud mist, is the majestic Absaroka/Beartooth Wilderness, famous for its high plateaus and hundreds of alpine lakes. At this high elevation the road is above timberline, over 10,000 feet. By July the ground is covered with flowers, especially various colored flocks. Back packers from around the country find this a favorite place to hike into and stay for several days. The trout species in these lakes vary, including the colorful golden trout which is only able to exist at elevations over 7000 feet.

BEARTOOTH MOUNTAINS
HELLROARING PLATEAU IN BACKGROUND

HIGH MOUNTAIN LAKES ON SOUTH SIDE OF THE PASS

Top photo - Looking south toward the Shoshone Mountains in Wyoming
Bottom photo - Alpine Lake, Absaroka/Beartooth Mountains

CHAPTER 3

HIGH MOUNTAIN LAKES

Absaroka-Beartooth and Crazy Mountains

Name	Drainage	Elevation	Acreage	Trailhead	Trout Species
Abandoned Lake	Clarks Fork	10100	10.5	Island Lake, Wyo	Brook
Albino Lake	Clarks Fork	10000	39.2	Island Lake, Wyo	Cutthroat
Alpine Lake	Boulder	8680	10.5	West Boulder #41	Cutthroat
Amphitheater Lake	Clarks Fork	9320	8.7	Clarks Fork	Brook
Anchor Lake	Clarks Fork	10045	12.0	Ivy Lake Jeep Tr	Golden
Anvil Lake	Stillwater	9440	10.1	Goose Lake Jeep Tr	Cutthroat
Aquarius Lake	Clarks Fork	9180	11.6	Clarks Fork	Cutthroat
Arch Lake	East Rosebud	10120	6.5	Alpine	Cutthroat
Arrapooash Lake	West Rosebud	9637	9.1	Mystic Lake #19	Cutthroat
Asteroid Lake	Stillwater	9380	3.2	Initial Creek,	Golden
Astral Lake	Clarks Fork	9320	5.2	Goose Lake Jeep Tr	Brook
Aufwuch Lake	Stillwater	8650	30.0	Woodbine	Cutthroat
Avalanche Lake	West Rosebud	9750	62.2	Mystic Lake	Cutthroat
Bald Knob Lake	Clarks Fork	9420	15.4	Clarks Fork	Brook
Barrier Lake	Stillwater	8150	42.4	West Stillwater Box Canyon	Rainbow
Beauty Lake	Stillwater	9200	5.9	Goose Lake Jeep Tr	Cutthroat
Beckwourth Lake	West Rosebud	9230	6.2	Mystic	Cutthroat
Big Butte Lake	Clarks Fork	10060	22.1	Moose Lake Jeep Tr	Golden
Big Moose Lake	Clarks Fork	8000	83.8	Clarks Fork	Rainbow
Big Park Lake	East Rosebud	8276	7.8	Alpine	Cutthroat
Bill Lake	Stillwater	8380	10.4	Woodbine	Cutthroat Brook

Courtesy of Montana Fish, Wildlife and Parks

Name	Drainage	Elevation	Acreage	Trailhead	Trout Species
Billy Lake	East Rosebud	10150	10.5	Alpine	Brook
Black Canyon Lake	Rock Creek	9280	82.4	Lake Fork Rock Creek	Cutthroat
Blacktail Lake	Boulder	8700	4.2	Davis Creek	Cutthroat
Blue Lake	Boulder	9460	10.2	Independence	Cutthroat
Bowback Lake	Rock Creek	10380	6.4	W Fork Rock Creek	Cutthroat
Bramble Lake #41	Boulder	9225	4.1	None	Cutthroat
Bridge Lake	Boulder	9585	14.2	Bridge Creek	Cutthroat
Broadwater Lake	Clarks Fork	8398	93.6	Clarks Fork	Brook
Burnt Bacon Lake	Clarks Fork	8950	15.0	Clay Butte	Grayling
Burnt Gulch Lake	Boulder	9040	9.1	Box Canyon	Cutthroat
Cairn Lake	East Rosebud	10186	148.3	Alpine	Brook
Camp Lake	Boulder	8995	7.8	Chrome Mtn	Cutthroat
Canyon Lake	Clarks Fork	8780	65.7	Clarks Fork	Cutthroat
Cataract Lake	Stillwater	8751	9.7	Woodbine	Cutthroat
Chickadee Lake	Boulder	9690	4.0	Upsidedown Tr	Cutthroat
Cimmerian Lake	Stillwater	8580	18.8	Box Canyon	Rainbow
Cliff Lake	Clarks Fork	9240	6.6	Initial Creek	Cutthroat
				Goose Lake Jeep Tr	Brook
				Lady Of The Lake 31	
Cliff Lake (Diamond)	Clarks Fork	8550	18.4	Clarks Fork	Grayling
Cloverleaf Lake 215	Clarks Fork	10170	18.4	Island Lake Wy	Cutthroat
Cloverleaf Lake 216	Clarks Fork	10180	23.9	Island Lake Wy	Cutthroat
Cloverleaf Lake 223	Clarks Fork	10150	31.0	Island Lake Wy	Cutthroat
Companion Lake	Clarks Fork	9415	5.2	Goose Lake Jeep Tr	Brook
Copeland Lake	Clarks Fork	8780	36.0	Ivy Lake Jeep Tr	Brook
Corner Lake	Clarks Fork	9220	11.1	Goose Lake Jeep Tr	Cutthroat
Courthouse Lake	Stillwater	10000	18.8	Goose Lake Jeep Tr	Cutthroat
Crescent Lake	Rock Creek	10000	13.6	Hellroaring Plateau	Brook
Crow Lake	East Rosebud	9064	11.4	Sylvan Lake 13	Brook
Crystal Lake	Clarks Fork	9910	27.5	Clay Butte	Cutthroat
Curl Lake	Clarks Fork	8398	30.6	Clarks Fork	Brook
Daly Lake	Rock Creek	9670	7.4	Hellroaring Plateau	Cutthroat
					Brook
Davis Lake	Boulder	8790	5.1	Davis Creek	Cutthroat
Desolation Lake	Clarks Fork	10155	31.4	Ivy Lake Jeep Tr	Golden
Dewey Lake	East Rosebud	9340	37.3	Alpine	Cutthroat
Diaphanous Lake	Stillwater	9631	9.2	Initial Creek	Rainbow
Dreary Lake	Stillwater	9040	15.5	Initial Creek	Rainbow
				Box Canyon Tr	
Dryad Lake	Stillwater	9090	5.1	Woodbine	Golden
				Box Canyon Tr	
Dude Lake	Rock Creek	10180	12.2	W Fork Rock Creek	Cutthroat
Duggan Lake	East Rosebud	8840	4.4	Alpine	Cutthroat
East Rosebud Lake	East Rosebud	6208	111.7	Alpine	Brown
					Rainbow
Echo Lake	East Rosebud	8486	12.2	Alpine	Cutthroat
Eedica Lake	West Rosebud	9720	8.9	Mystic Lake	Cutthroat
Elk Lake	East Rosebud	6780	7.3	Alpine	Brook
Elk Lake	Boulder	9580	9.2	Copper Creek	Cutthroat
Emerald Lake	Rock Creek	9750	39.2	Glacier Lake	Brook
					Cutthroat
Emerald Lake	West Rosebud	6310	28.5	W Rosebud	Brook
					Rainbow

51

Name	Drainage	Elevation	Acreage	Trailhead	Trout Species
Estelle Lake	Clarks Fork	9200	18.7	Clay Butte	Brook
Falls Creek Lake	Boulder	8942	39.7	Fourmile	Cutthroat
				Spectacular Creek	
Farley Lake	Clarks Fork	9740	24.0	Ivy Lake Jeep Tr	Brook
				Crazy Creek	
Favonius Lake	Stillwater	9410	25.5	Box Canyon	Cutthroat
Felis Lake	Clarks Fork	10440	17.5	Island Lake Wy	Cutthroat
First Rock Lake	Rock Creek	8870	17.5	Lake Fork Rock Creek	Brook
					Cutthroat
Fish Lake	Boulder	9472	18.0	Box Canyon	Cutthroat
				Upsidedown Creek	Cutthroat
Flat Rock Lake	Clarks Fork	9990	37.0	Clay Butte	Cutthroat
				Muddy Creek	
Forsaken Lake	Clarks Fork	10450	30.5	Clay Butte	Cutthroat
				Muddy Creek	
Fossil Lake	East Rosebud	9900	164.7	Clarks Fork	Cutthroat
				Alpine	
Fox Lake	Clarks Fork	8065	111.4	Clarks Fork	Brook
					Rainbow
Fenco Lake	West Rosebud	9115	13.9	Mystic Lake	Cutthroat
Froze To Death Lake	East Rosebud	10156	74.5	Phantom Creek	Cutthroat
Gallery Lake	Clarks Fork	9920	7.4	Clarks Fork 3	Rainbow
Glacier Creek Lake	Stillwater	8920	16.3	Goose Lake Jeep Tr	Brook
Glacier Lake	Rock Creek	9702	176.0	Glacier Lake	Cutthroat
Golden Lake	Clarks Fork	10130	48.9	Island Lake Wy	Cutthroat
Goose Lake	Stillwater	9830	102.0	Goose Lake Jeep Tr	Cutthroat
Granite Lake	Clarks Fork	8625	228.0	Clay Butte	Brook
				Muddy Creek	Rainbow
Great Falls Creek Lake	Boulder	9452	6.6	Great Falls Creek	Rainbow
Green Lake	Clarks Fork	9640	35.7	Clay Butte	Brook
				Crazy Lakes	
Gus Lake	Clarks Fork	9890	16.7	Island Lake Wy	Brook
Hairpin Lake	Rock Creek	10160	32.9	Hellroaring Plateau	Cutthroat
Heather Lake	Slough Creek	9275	4.4	Lake Abundance	Cutthroat
Heidi Lake	Clarks Fork	9720	8.2	Clay Butte	Brook
				Muddy Creek	
Hellroaring Lake	Rock Creek	10160	32.9	Hellroaring Plateau	Cutthroat
Hidden Lake	Clarks Fork	9500	18.0	Clarks Fork	Cutthroat
Hipshot Lake	Clarks Fork	9650	9.6	Clarks Fork	Cutthroat
Horseshoe Lake	Boulder	9490	15.9	Upsidedown Tr	Cutthroat
Huckleberry Lake	Stillwater	9520	15.3	Goose Lake Jeep Tr	Rainbow
Hunger Lake	Clarks Fork	9655	5.1	Goose Lake Jeep Tr	Brook
Icicle	Boulder	9465	6.7	West Boulder	Rainbow
Imelda Lake	Stillwater	9750	32.4	Lake Abundance	Brook
Incisor Lake	Stillwater	9640	5.9	Goose Lake Jeep Tr	Golden
Indian Knife Lake	Clarks Fork	9740	5.3	Clarks Fork	Brook
Island Lake	West Rosebud	7717	144.0	Mystic Lake	Rainbow
Jasper Lake	Clarks Fork	10150	54.8	Island Lake Wy	Cutthroat
Jay Lake	Stillwater	9600	23.7	Woodbine	Cutthroat
				Initial Creek	
Jordan Lake	Stillwater	8970	14.7	Box Canyon	Cutthroat
Jordan Lake	Clarks Fork	9625	36.0	Clarks Fork	Cutthroat
Kaufman Lake	Boulder	8942	39.7	Fourmile	Cutthroat
				Speculator Creek	

Name	Drainage	Elevation	Acreage	Trailhead	Trout Species
Kersey Lake	Clarks Fork	8070	118.0	Clarks Fork	Brook
					Lake
					Cutthroat
Keyser Brown	Rock Creek	8720	9.5	Lake Fork Rock Creek	Brook
					Cutthroat
Kookoo Lake	Rock Creek	10200	6.1	West Fork Rock Creek	Cutthroat
Lady Of The Lake	Clarks Fork	8800	42.8	Lady Of The Lake	Brook
Lake Abundance	Slough Creek	8400	17.2	Lake Abundance	Cutthroat
Lake At Falls	East Rosebud	8100	49.8	Alpine	Cutthroat
Lake Columbine	Boulder	9132	5.3	Box Canyon	Grayling
Lake Elaine	Clarks Fork	9250	132.4	Clay Butte	Brook
Lake Gertrude	Rock Creek	9550	6.1	Timberline	Brook
Lake Mary	Rock Creek	9330	8.0	West Fork Rock Creek	Brook
Lake Mcknight	Boulder	9120	10.8	Davis Creek	Golden
Lake Of The Clouds	Clarks Fork	9680	23.6	Clarks Fork	Cutthroat
Lake Of The Winds	Clarks Fork	9910	40.7	Clarks Fork	Cutthroat
Lake Of The Woods	Stillwater	8675	7.9	Lake Abundance	Cutthroat
Lake Pinchot	Stillwater	9260	53.9	Upsidedown Creek	Rainbow
				Box Canyon	
Lake Surrender	Stillwater	8625	9.1	Box Canyon	Rainbow
				West Stillwater	Cutthroat
Lake Wilderness	Stillwater	9481	19.0	Near Chrome Lake	Cutthroat
Leaky Raft Lake	Clarks Fork	10150	8.5	Goose Lake Jeep Tr	Cutthroat
Lea Lake	Clarks Fork	9300	8.5	Clarks Fork	Cutthroat
Lightning Lake	Stillwater	9340	61.3	Initial Creek	Golden
Line Lake	Clarks Fork	9680	4.7	Near Mt-Wy Border	Cutthroat
Little Face Lake	West Rosebud	9980	8.4	Mystic Lake	Cutthroat
Little Falls Lake	Clarks Fork	9620	11.4	Clay Butte	Brook
Little Goose Lake	Stillwater	9835	8.1	Goose Lake Jeep Tr	Cutthroat
Little Lightning Lake	Stillwater	9280	6.9	Initial Creek	Golden
Little Scat Lake	East Rosebud	9330	5.0	Alpine	Golden
Lone Elk Lake	Clarks Fork	10070	18.1	Goose Lake Jeep Tr	Brook
				Lady Of The Lake	Grayling
Lonesome Lake	Clarks Fork	10050	35.3	Island Lake	Brook
Long Lake	Clarks Fork	9471	11.9	Goose Lake Jeep Tr	Brook
Lost Lake	Rock Creek	8520	11.3	Lake Fork Rock Creek	Grayling
					Cutthroat
Lower Aero Lake	Clarks Fork	9995	189.9	Goose Lake Jeep Tr	Brook
				Lady Of The Lake	Cutthroat
Lower Arch Crk Lake	East Rosebud	9580	24.3	Alpine	Cutthroat
Lower Snow Lake	East Rosebud	9160	8.0	Alpine	Rainbow
Lower Storm Lake	West Rosebud	9839	17.8	Mystic Lake	Cutthroat
Mariane Lake	Clarks Fork	9542	50.8	Clarks Fork	Brook
Marker Lake	Rock Creek	10870	15.5	W Fork Rock Creek	Cutthroat
Martes Lake	Stillwater	9150	17.5	Box Canyon Tr 27	Cutthroat
Martin Lake	Clarks Fork	9660	31.4	Clay Butte	Brook
Martin Lake	East Rosebud	9260	30.0	Alpine	Golden
Medicine Lake	East Rosebud	9906	30.3	Alpine	Cutthroat
Mermaid Lake	Clarks Fork	9700	6.8	Clarks Fork	Cutthroat
Midnight Lake	Clarks Fork	9480	5.1	Ivy Lake Jeep Tr	Brook
Mirror Lake	Boulder	9740	16.4	Upsidedown Tr	Rainbow
Moccasin Lake	Clarks Fork	9400	6.8	Goose Lake Jeep Tr	Brook
Moon Lake	Rock Creek	10400	82.2	Glacier Lake	Cutthroat

Name	Drainage	Elevation	Acreage	Trailhead	Trout Species
Mountain Goat Lake	Rock Creek	10040	12.5	Glacier Lake	Cutthroat
Mountain Sheep Lake	Rock Creek	9985	7.3	Glacier Lake	Cutthroat
Mountain View Lake	Stillwater	6750	4.0	Horseman Flats	Brook White Sucker
Mouse Lake	Stillwater	9650	6.9	Box Canyon Woodbine	Cutthroat
Mystic Lake	West Rosebud	7673	435.0	Mystic Lake	Rainbow
Narrow Escape Lake	Boulder	9340	11.6	Upsidedown Creek Box Canyon	Cutthroat
Nemidji Lake	West Rosebud	9595	13.7	Mystic Lake	Cutthroat
North Picket Pin Lake	Stillwater	8825	5.3	Picket Pin Rd	Cutthroat
Nugget Lake	West Rosebud	9340	8.3	W Rosebud	Cutthroat
Otter Lake	Clarks Fork	9620	61.2	Clarks Fork	Grayling Brook
Ovis Lake	Clarks Fork	9600	8.6	Goose Lake Jeep Tr	Cutthroat
Owl Lake	Stillwater	9541	14.4	Upsidedown Tr	Cutthroat
Peace Lake	Slough Creek	8725	4.7	Independence Lake Abundance	Cutthroat
Pentad Lake	Stillwater	9362	40.7	Box Canyon	Cutthroat
Phantom Lake	East Rosebud	9320	19.5	Phantom Creek	Cutthroat
Picasso Lake	Clarks Fork	9800	8.1	Clarks Fork	Golden
Pipit Lake	Stillwater	9580	7.0	Upsidedown Tr	Cutthroat
Princess Lake	West Rosebud	9080	25.0	Mystic Lake	Cutthroat
Prospect Lake	Boulder	9640	6.8	Fourmile Ranger St	Cutthroat
Queer Lake	Clarks Fork	9600	26.4	Clay Butte	Brook
Rainbow Lakes (7)	Boulder	9395	Very	Box Canyon Upsidedown Creek	Rainbow
Ram Lake	West Rosebud	9580	14.4	West Rosebud	Cutthroat
Raven Lake	Stillwater	8750	10.0	Box Canyon W Stillwater	Rainbow Cutthroat
Recruitment Lake	Clarks Fork	10038	13.1	Goose Lake Jeep Tr	Brook
Renie Lake	Clarks Fork	9900	15.3	Clay Butte	Brook
Rimrock Lake	East Rosebud	7540	33.6	Alpine	Rainbow
Robin Lake	Clarks Fork	9575	8.3	Clay Butte	Brook
Rock Island Lake	Clarks Fork	8166	137.0	Clarks Fork	Brook Cutthroat
Rock Tree Lake	Clarks Fork	9820	18.1	Clarks Fork	Golden
Rough Lake	Clarks Fork	10150	102.2	Goose Lake Jeep Tr Lady Of The Lake	Grayling Brook
Round Lake	Clarks Fork	9340	31.0	Goose Lake Jeep Tr	Brook Cutthroat
Russel Lake	Clarks Fork	8780	27.5	Clarks Fork	Brook
Saderbalm Lake	Stillwater	8980	7.4	Initial Creek Horsemen Flats	Grayling
Scat Lake	East Rosebud	9310	7.0	Alpine	Golden
Second Rock Lake	Rock Creek	9110	25.9	Lake Fork Rock Creek	Brook
Sedge Lake	Clarks Fork	9100	4.7	Clarks Fork	Cutthroat
September Morn lake	Rock Creek	9696	11.3	Lake Fork Rock Creek	Brook
Shadow Lake	East Rosebud	8400	8.4	Armstrong Creek	Brook
Shelf Lake	Rock Creek	10120	51.0	Glacier Lake	Brook
Shelter Lake	Clarks Fork	10040	6.8	Goose Lake Jeep Tr Lady Of The Lake	Brook
Ship Lake	Rock Creek	10400	28.9	West Fork Rock Creek	Brook

ABOVE TIMBERLINE, HIGH IN THE ROCKY MOUNTAINS

IN THE MONTHS OF JUNE, JULY AND AUGUST, WATER IS FLOWING EVERYWHERE

SMALL WATER CASCADES AND QUAINT LITTLE STREAMS ARE ABUNDANT

HIGH MOUNTAIN STREAMS

ROCKY MOUNTAIN WILD FLOWERS

Name	Drainage	Elevation	Acreage	Trailhead	Trout Species
Silt Lake #2	Rock Creek	9800	4.4	West Fork Rock Creek	Cutthroat
Silver Lake	Boulder	9046	10.0	Fourmile Creek	Rainbow
Silver Lake	West Rosebud	7820	72.6	Mystic Lake	Rainbow Cutthroat
Skeeter Lake	Clarks Fork	9310	10.7	Clay Butte Crazy Lakes	Grayling
Skull Lake	Clarks Fork	9640	5.5	Clarks Fork	Brook
Sliderock Lake	Rock Creek	10480	81.0	Hellroaring Plateau	Brook
Silver Lake	Clarks Fork	9520	6.9	Goose Lake Jeep Tr	Brook
Slough Lake	East Rosebud	7500	5.8	Phantom Creek	Brook
Smethurst Lake	Rock Creek	9580	4.6	Hellroaring Plateau	Brook Cutthroat
Snowbank Lake	Rock Creek	10040	18.8	Hellroaring Plateau	Brook
Sodalite Lake	Clarks Fork	9840	25.8	Clarks Fork	Brook
South Picket Pin Lake	Stillwater	9025	5.0	Picket Pin Road	Cutthroat
Spaghetti Lake	Clarks Fork	9190	6.3	Clay Butte Crazy Lakes	Grayling
Speculator Lake	Boulder	9449	9.7	Fourmile Creek Speculator Creek	Cutthroat
Spider Lake	Stillwater	9750	6.3	Goose Lake Jeep Tr	Brook
Squeeze Lake	Boulder	9535	7.0	Upsidedown Tr Box Canyon Tr	Cutthroat
Star Lake	Clarks Fork	9646	7.9	Goose Lake Jeep Tr	Cutthroat
Star Lake	West Rosebud	8640	23.5	Mystic Lake	Cutthroat
Stephanie Lake	Clarks Fork	10260	13.9	Clarks Fork	Cutthroat
Summerville Lake	Clarks Fork	9560	43.0	Clay Butte	Brook
Sundown Lake	Stillwater	9500	5.2	Box Canyon Tr Woodbine	Cutthroat
Sunken Rock Lake	Stillwater	9250	11.0	Box Canyon Tr Woodbine	Golden
Surprise Lake	Clarks Fork	9860	7.1	Goose Lake Jeep Tr Lady Of The Lake	Cutthroat
Swamp Lake	Clarks Fork	8900	10.4	Lady Of The Lake	Cutthroat
Swede Lake	Clarks Fork	9810	11.8	Clay Butte Muddy Creek	Cutthroat
Sylvan Lake	East Rosebud	9165	18.5	Sylvan Lake	Golden
Tiel Lake	Clarks Fork	9260	18.5	Clay Butte	Brook
Timberline Lake	Rock Creek	9660	31.4	Timberline	Brook
Trail Lake	Clarks Fork	9800	7.1	Clay Butte	Cutthroat
Triangle Lake	Rock Creek	9730	7.9	Glacier Lake	Cutthroat
Triangle Lake	Clarks Fork	9830	6.3	Clarks Fork	Cutthroat
Triangle Lake	Rock Creek	10440	6.3	West Fork Rock Creek	Cutthroat
Tumble Lake	Stillwater	9080	53.2	Initial Creek	Cutthroat
Turgulse Lake	East Rosebud	10206	82.9	Phantom Creek	Cutthroat
Twin Outlets Lake	East Rosebud	9190	29.5	Alpine	Cutthroat
Upper Aero Lake	Clarks Fork	10140	291.8	Goose Lake Jeep Tr Lady Of The Lake	Cutthroat
Upper Arch Creek Lake	East Rosebud	10120	46.9	Alpine	Cutthroat
Upper Basin Creek	Rock Creek	8960	6.7	Basin Creek	Brook
Upper Snow Lake	East Rosebud	9265	10.4	Alpine	Rainbow
Vernon Lake	Clarks Fork	7900	8.2	Clarks Fork	Brook Cutthroat
W Fishtail Cr Lake	West Rosebud	9690	7.3	Benbow Mine	Golden

Name	Drainage	Elevation	Acreage	Trailhead	Trout Species
Wade Lake	Clarks Fork	9620	10.5	Ivy Lake Jeep Tr	Brook
Wall Lake	Clarks Fork	9900	14.4	Clay Butte	Brook
Weasel Lake	Boulder	9440	8.6	Great Falls Creek	Cutthroat
Wednesday Lake	Clarks Fork	10200	6.2	Island Lake Wy	Cutthroat
Weeluna Lake	West Rosebud	9694	10.2	Mystic Lake	Cutthroat
West Boulder Lake	Boulder	9628	13.0	Fourmile Creek	Cutthroat
West Rosebud Lake	West Rosebud	6387	19.0	Drive To	Brook Brown Rainbow
Widewater Lake	Clarks Fork	8008	110.7	Clarks Fork	Brook Rainbow
Wiedy Lake	Clarks Fork	9010	7.0	Lady Of The Lake	Cutthroat
Windy Lake	Clarks Fork	9830	36.7	Clarks Fork	Brook
Wood Lake	Stillwater	9690	12.0	Near Chrome Lake	Cutthroat

CHAPTER 4
WATERFALLS AND CASCADES

WOODBINE FALLS

WOODBINECANYON CASCADE

WATERFALLS AND CASCADES

Western and southern Montana contain some of the most beautiful and majestic waterfalls in America some accessible by road.

NATURAL BRIDGE WATERFALL

This is a very beautiful and unique waterfall that is located on the main fork of the Boulder river, about thirty miles south of Big Timber which is on Interstate 90. . It gets its name from the fact that the river upstream flows into a large hole in its bottom and emerges out the side of a rock wall at the falls. Thus it has what you might call a "natural bridge". The water actually comes out in three places, one large outlet and two smaller ones. In the spring during runoff the heavy flow of water causes some to go over the bridge. It is not surprising that many a photographer has tried to capture the beauty of it on film. I consider myself a pretty good amateur, and I have tried to do it justice in film, but was disappointed when I got the pictures.

To add to the beauty, the falls drops into a swirling hole that circles under a large rock mass overhang, and then moves white-water fast through a deep canyon. It is well into the mountains making for one breathtaking scene.

The falls serves as a dividing line as to the type of trout available. Above the falls the trout are primarily rainbows and cutthroat. Below the falls are mostly browns and rainbows. In the area the fish are mostly ten to twelve inches in size and appear to be well fed.

Going back downstream a few miles north is the small community of McCloud where one can get fishing supplies and rent a modest cabin. There is a campground nearby and others north of the falls.

CRAZY CREEK CASCADE

This is a gorgeous long cascade that is right off the highway going toward the northeast entrance to Yellowstone Park. During spring runoff it presents quite a roar as it passes over large boulders and sloping rock masses It is practically right on the Montana-Wyoming border on state highway 212 which crisscrosses the state line in the area. If you hope to fish the stream, you will need a Wyoming fishing license.

CRAZY CREEK CASCADE

This beautiful and loud cascade is located near the northeast entrance to Yellowstone Park, just a short walking distance from highway 212. It flows out of the Absaroka/Beartooth Range into the Clark's Fork River, an excellent trout stream.

A short distance west the highway crosses back into Montana. Running along the highway in this area are the upper waters of the Clark's Fork river which Crazy Creek runs into.

WOODBINE FALLS

When traveling along the upper waters of the Stillwater river, you come across this falls that is high up on the mountainside to the east on the other side of the river from the road. It is made up of two falls, one below the other. At the base of the mountain is a campground from which a trail leads to the falls. It is somewhat of a hike, but is worth the effort. At the campground there are fairly good fishing and camping facilities.

WOODBINE CASCADE

This is a favorite hike of many outdoors enthusiasts. At high water you cannot hear yourself think while walking the trail as it goes through a deep gorge that goes for most of a mile. At the head of it, just above the gorge, is a beautiful meadow that has a lake with brook trout. The fish are not very large but big enough to eat. From this point one can do a three or four day hike, if equipped for it, all the way to Cook City near Yellowstone Park and enjoy good fishing along the way.

HIGH MOUNTAIN WATERFALLS (ABOVE TIMBERLINE)

Waterfalls and cascades in the upper plateaus of the southern Montana mountains are plentiful. But it is necessary to do extensive hiking to see them. The top of the beautiful Absaroka-Beartooth range southwest of Billings can be reached by a scary road that ends at the Hellroaring Plateau. This is where the hiking begins and if you are especially ambitious you can hike above 10000 feet passing dozens of lakes and cascades for about 30 miles to the west.

In the East Rosebud drainage is a lake called Lake-at-the -Falls. It is called this, naturally, because a waterfall drops into it. Beautiful scenery to say the least. On up the drainage is another beautiful waterfall.

UPPER AND LOWER MESA FALLS

Just beyond the far Southwest Montana border into Idaho are the two Mesa falls. The upper Mesa is a beautiful waterfall that is shaped like a curtain and is difficult to get a good look at   It is particularly beautiful in the fall when it is surrounded by the a variety of vibrant colors.

NATURAL BRIDGE FALLS
DURING SPRING RUNOFF THE RIVER FLOWS OVER THE TOP

WOODBINE FALLS
HIGH ABOVE THE STILLWATER RIVER

CHAPTER 5

THE SPECIES OF TROUT AND THEIR HABITS

THE SPECIES OF TROUT AND THEIR HABITS

The most predominant trout in Southern Montana are the brown and rainbow trout, but in recent years there has been a push to populate various lakes and streams with the cutthroat trout. The brook trout is also found in various waters in the state, but it does not live long compared to the others. In the western part of the state there are grayling in some streams. All of these fish are of the *salmonid* family. The white fish, which does not look like a trout, is also of this family. There are other kinds of trout but the five mentioned are the most common in southern Montana. Nonetheless, we will consider all of the different trout currently populating streams in the area.

There are certain characteristics of trout that are basically common to all the species. At one time it was said that they are color blind, but now it is common knowledge that color does make a difference. Spin fishing with the daredevil lure is a case in point. I have had much more success with the brass daredevil than with the silver or copper. Some anglers who like to stroll on lakes have told me that it helps to add a lot of color to their cowbells or whatever they are using.

Trout are easily spooked and once they are, they will not strike for a time. If fishing in a small stream, like a spring creek, it is important to stay out of their range or angle of vision. Keep from making too much noise, and wear clothing that blends in with the background.

They tend to feed on whatever happens to be available. If a particular hatch is taking place, that emerging fly is what they feed on and tend to ignore anything else in or on the water. Anglers will usually get best results using a corresponding replica of the insect.

Early morning and late evening seem to be the best time to catch them. This may be because they have not fed all night, and at sunup, they are hungry. However, nights with a bright moon can be an exception to this. After a nap they begin feeding again later in the day. This is not a hard and fast rule because there have been times I made some good catches during midday. Although some fishermen quit when it starts to rain, at times this can produce good results. This is good reason to keep a rain jacket on hand.

There is an indicator of what the trout are feeding on. It is the manner in which they are feeding as evidenced by the bulge, ripple, or splash they cause on the surface. This is called *reading the rise*. A lot of splashing is indicative of a hatch such as that of the mayfly or stonefly. A bulge or ripple may mean they are feeding on insects just under the surface, possibly emergers. My personal experience is that in most mountain streams, it is difficult to discern anything from this phenomenon. Whatever the case, one may select a fly based on this if it is discernible.

The growth of trout is affected by a number of factors: the size of the river, water temperature, limestone minerals, and amount and type of insects and other food in the water. Limestone minerals affect the PH factor of the water, causing it to be less acidic, which is better for trout growth. Trout remain fairly small in streams in the mountains where the water is colder and food less abundant. In the bigger rivers, there is often larger types of food such as crustaceans. Below dams the water is a more constant temperature, which makes for more insects and other food on and under the surface of the water.

Another factor that has a bearing on when and where fishermen go and what they use for bait is the spawning. The larger females loaded with eggs will migrate upstream to spawn. At some location they lay their eggs in a burrowed space in the bottom called a redd. They are somewhat easier to catch at this time.

Trout spawn at different times as follows:

Brown	Fall
Rainbow	Spring
Cutthroat	Spring
Brook	Early Fall
Greyling	Spring

Each trout has its own distinctive habits as discussed in the following pages.

BROWN TROUT

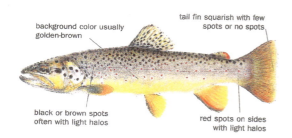

background color usually golden-brown

tail fin squarish with few spots or no spots

black or brown spots often with light halos

red spots on sides with light halos

This creature is considered by many, including myself, the hardiest and most exciting of the trout species. They are present in just about all the streams and most lakes, and can survive to a very large size. They are known to exist in other parts of the world, such as Europe and South America.

 The origin of the brown is Germany and thus it is often called the German brown. It has also been called the loch leven which has its origin in England, or more specifically, Scotland. These two species no doubt have a common origin because no veteran angler I have known seems to really know the difference between the two, and the distinguishing marks and colors are very similar. German brown and loch leven have basically become synonymous. Some experts say it has the longest life span of all the trout, and some go as far as to say it is the smartest..

Contrary to the rainbow, the brown has more of an appetite for insects under the surface. In many of the streams, their favorite food is the stone fly larvae that is 100 percent protein. After the hatch has run its course, sometime in June, it will seek other food in the water. This larvae would be a very healthy food, even for humans. They grow and exist under the rocks in fairly fast, but shallow, water until they hatch. The browns love them and will move rocks to get at them. This is why, as they get older, if they survive, their snout becomes distorted and stubby. You do not see this in the rainbows. If it had to choose between a grasshopper, worm, or stone fly larvae, it would be the latter. Some sources say the larger browns even have an appetite for rainbow minnows.

As browns get large they are not as out in the open as other trout, preferring to hang out under sunken logs, undercut banks, and branches hanging out over the water. Their feeding times are different, oftentimes feeding at night unlike other species. Their favorite food, when available, are the larvae of may flies, caddis flies, and especially the stone fly. When the streams are at high water, clear or murky, there is usually a lot of food in the water, and they linger near the banks. Since the water is not moving so fast, there is more likely to be insects coming off the bank. So when fishing for them at this time, it is best to cast the bait into holes along the bank. Tied flies are not particularly good in high water, especially if murky, because there is just too much food under the surface.

As browns get large, they tend to look for larger food such as minnows, frogs, mice, and, in some streams, crawfish. I witnessed my father catching a five pound brown that looked pregnant. In an unusually expanded stomach, it had a frog, mouse, and two minnows, one being about 6 inches. Actually, it is rare to find these items in the stomach of a large fish, but there will usually be a lot of the larger type insects such as the stone fly larvae, and less frequently, the grasshopper. Thus in high water, I usually use one of these for bait. The most attractive grasshopper is the large one we call the "green top", having a green top shell with a yellow bottom. In the spring or early summer before the stone fly hatch, I have opened the belly of a large fish and found it stuffed to capacity with stone fly larvae. When hoppers are in season, some of them my be in the belly..

Where these fish hang out in the water is discussed in the chapter "Reading The Water". When the streams begin to come down and become more clear, food is not as plentiful in the water. They will then begin to feed off the surface more, and thus, you turn to flies, especially dry flies.

The best time to fish for browns is in the fall when they are spawning because the larger females are moving up stream to lay their eggs. During this time they are easier to catch. It seems they are more responsive to lures, whether they are going after them to eat or possibly fight them.

The brown is considered by many to be much hardier than other trout. It can stand a greater range of water temperatures and PH factor, and are more self sustaining compared to other trout.

It has been noticed that the brown does often break water when hooked, sometimes jumping quite high. However, the larger ones seem to prefer going down into underwater brush or branches to tangle the line, in which case the fisherman needs to steer it away. Or it will head into fast water, in which case, an experienced angler will need to go with it to keep from too much pull on the line. If the tension exceeds the strength of the leader, goodbye fish!

When you first pull a brown from the water, at this moment, it is the most beautiful. I am always impressed with the blend of colors: green top, brown and yellow sides, and orange or red spots. They also make a nice healthy meal. To start a day off right, when you are camping by the stream, it is suggested you fry them over a fire, and serve them with hash browns and eggs.

RAINBOW TROUT

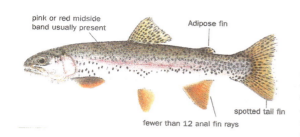

pink or red midside
band usually present

Adipose fin

spotted tail fin

fewer than 12 anal fin rays

These beautiful creatures have the coloring consistent with their name. Along the middle of their silvery sides are hues of pink, blue and green. Most of the streams in southern Montana contain them, but they seem to prefer colder and, at times, faster water than other species.

If you catch one in the spring, you will probably find eggs inside. While flies are always good bait for them, spinners can be more effective during spawning. Theory has it that because they are spawning, they may be fighting the lure rather than seeking it for food. If a lure is dropped right on top of one of them, it is more likely to strike. However, trout fishermen prefer to go after rainbows with flies because they are more of a surface feeder.

Rainbows come very large on the Big Horn River, and are more readily seen in the water when spawning in the spring. An interesting phenomena, unique with the Big Horn, is that the spawning rainbows draw close to anglers wading, because food is stirred up off the bottom. The spawning season draws a big crowd of anglers from all over, but there are plenty of fish to go around. The Montana Fish, Wildlife & Parks (MFW&P) reports that the trout population in the river can be as high as 8,000 per mile. This is sustained partly because it is primarily catch-and-release to all except the Crow Indians. The river runs through their reservation.

What many anglers like about the rainbow is its tendency to jump sometimes amazingly high in the air. I have had them go for my fly before it hit the water. Ordinarily, trout will feed in calmer water, but the rainbow is sometimes caught in fast water, to the surprise of the angler. I have even snagged them in white water, catching me completely off guard. One would suspect that they develop more strength than other trout due to this characteristic, which may be why they clear the water at times by several feet. They also seem to enjoy water with a ripple surface, as do the other trout.

The colors of this beautiful fish are truly striking, a mixture of what is seen in a real rainbow in the clouds during or after a rain. Blue and pink on bright silvery sides speckled with dark green spots is a challenge to any artist trying to duplicate it. Rainbows, like the brown, will sometimes gorge themselves if there is plenty of food in the water.

One time as a teenager while fishing the Yellowstone with the County Sheriff, I was faced with helping him land a huge rainbow trout, what looked to be at least eight or ten pounds. He was standing on the bank between two trees that prohibited him from going to a spot where he could land it. I was able to get down to the water just below him with a net   It appeared to me the net was too small but he said go for it anyway. I did manage to net the fish but it was too large, possibly 12 to 15 pounds, and it just flopped out of the net and broke the line. The sheriff never took me fishing again.

Sometimes when you land a rainbow you might notice a redness around the gills. This is an indication that it is a high bred cross between a rainbow and a cutthroat. This fish seems to be even more high-spirited than the rainbow itself. They can be found in many of the rivers in southern Montana.

BROOK TROUT

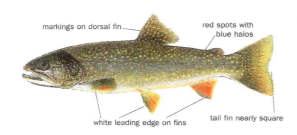

This, too, is a beautiful fish with its own distinctive colors and markings. It has deep reddish brown sides with red and black spots and a yellowish bottom. It is most colorful just after pulling it from the water. It has a short life span of about three to five years, shorter than the brown trout

In general they are small, usually less than eight inches, and are easy to catch. In some environments they can get quite large.   To find more "brookies", as they are called, it is usually necessary to fish in the upper waters of streams or lakes in the mountains.   In essence, they prefer clear fresh water as opposed to the more polluted or murkier water of rivers away from the mountains. They are related to the bull trout, and can hybridize with them, however, the bull trout has become very rare.

Because their habitat is the smaller streams where food in the water is scarce, they do not get near as big as the brown or rainbow. Some say that in some bodies of water they are small because they reproduce rapidly to the point that there is not enough food to go around. The largest I have caught was about one and a half pounds, although, in some foreign countries such as Argentina there are some that weigh over four pounds. In Montana I have went into difficult areas to get them and the largest I caught was about 10 inches. The state record is slightly over nine pounds, caught out of a lake in 1940.

They seem to like calm water in streams such as around beaver dams, and that is where I have had the best success catching them. Sioux Charley Lake, above Woodbine Canyon on the Stillwater river, is loaded with them, and they are easy to catch. Also, the upper waters of the Big Hole River in southwestern Montana have them. Overall, they are not as plentiful and not as easy to find as brown and rainbow trout.

In their efforts to reestablish the cutthroat trout, the MFW&P has is some places had to remove the brook trout first. They say, they are one "pesky" fish to get rid of very easily. With much effort, however, it is getting done.

If one plans to make a trip into Montana to fish for the brook trout, the trip could possibly be disappointing, due to the remoteness of places to catch them. Nonetheless, if you catch one, you have to admit, it is one beautiful fish.

CUTTHROAT TROUT

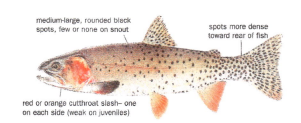

medium-large, rounded black spots, few or none on snout

spots more dense toward rear of fish

red or orange cutthroat slash– one on each side (weak on juveniles)

This is the native trout of Yellowstone Park and southcentral Montana, and therefore is called the yellowstone cutthroat. For decades the famous Fishing Bridge in the park has been a tourist attraction because you can stand on the bridge and look down at nice size cutthroat trout in the water.

The lake was at one time teeming with them. However, in recent years, lake trout somehow got into the lake and have been feeding on them causing a significant drop in the population. Now there is a program to get rid of the lake trout and restore the cutthroat. As of 2012 it is still an ongoing project which is proving to be difficult.

As with the other trout, the cutthroat has beautiful distinctive colors and markings. Two outstanding characteristics are the light greenish color on the sides and the reddish markings on the gills, thus the name cutthroat.

There has been an effort to introduce them into more of the streams and lakes of southern Montana, even going so far as to replace rainbow, brown and brook trout in some places. Cutthroat have crossbred with the rainbow trout, and this is why sometimes you catch a rainbow that has the reddish gills. Of course, it is a hybrid, unable to reproduce. It is the intention of the MFW&P to greatly increase the cutthroat population in the state and inhibit crossbreeding with the rainbow. In some lakes where they have hybridized, the MFW&P is swamping out the rainbow genes by continual stocking of the cutthroat. The objective is to get the pure cutthroat back. For some, the pure yellowstone cutthroat seems to be the trout of choice over all the others. At this time cutthroat are only catch and release.

GOLDEN TROUT

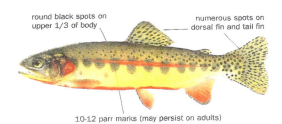

round black spots on upper 1/3 of body

numerous spots on dorsal fin and tail fin

10-12 parr marks (may persist on adults)

In order to catch one of these, you will need to plan on hiking into a high mountain lake. That is the only place to find them, but some anglers feel it is worth the effort. This species takes the trophy for beauty with its gold and red colors..

Similar to the brook trout they are very seldom more than two pounds. The state record catch is 5.4 pounds. There have been reports that in some high lakes, though not in Montana, they reach several pounds. These delicate trout normally need to be in a lake over 7000 feet elevation, or above timberline, in crystal clear cold water, to survive. One such lake is Sylvan Lake that can be reached through the East Rosebud Lake drainage. (See the chapter *Southern Montana Lakes*) It requires a difficult hike to get there. If it is your desire to make such a trip, you might consider one of the outfitters in Montana who will take you in by horseback. If you want to go in on foot, lacking experience at backpacking, it may be best to go in along with someone who is experienced. When you arrive there, you will be glad you made the effort because it has some nice 13 inch golden trout

BULL TROUT

In my forty some years of fishing in Montana, I have caught only one . It had a lamprey stuck to its side which, in time, would kill the fish. (The lamprey is a blood sucking predator that is about a foot long and shaped like an eel with a mouth like a funnel lined with teeth. It clamps onto the side of a fish). The bull trout has become very few in number. Not much is known about them except now and then you hear of someone catching one.

GRAYLING

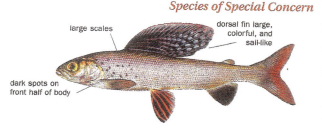

large scales

dorsal fin large, colorful, and sail-like

dark spots on front half of body

This fish has much the same shape as the trout except it has a high dorsal fin and a smaller mouth. It is a member of the salmonid family which also includes trout. The only one I have caught was out of Ennis lake in southwestern Montana.

At first when I hooked it, I thought I had a bird on the end of the line. These fish can jump higher than any of the trout, and put up a very hard fight. They do not have the beautiful colors of the trout, but a rather plain silvery color. This fish is scarce in Montana except for the western part of the state. One place they can be found is in the upper waters of the Big Hole River in the southwest corner of the state. They are abundant in Alaska.

WHITEFISH

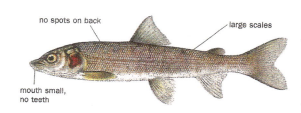

no spots on back

large scales

mouth small, no teeth

This fish prefers cold water, and is often found in the same streams inhabited by trout. It is part of the *salmonid* family. They are not as eatable as the trout, as the bones are much smaller and hard to separate from the meat. For this reason it has been called the "Montana bone fish".

It has a much smaller mouth than the trout, and is always white in color, thus the name. Because of the small mouth, they go after flies. When hooked, they put up a pretty good fight, but are seldom over two pounds.

Some anglers like to fish for them on the Yellowstone River in the winter when it is partially frozen over. They use a fly reel and a 10-12 foot bamboo rod that reaches out over the ice and with maggots for bait.

CHAPTER 6
TROUT FISHING EQUIPMENT & ACCESSORIES

FLY FISHING

The Fly Rod and Reel

To get started fly fishing, the first order of business is to get the rod and reel. Those who want to get serious about it need to get a high quality rod that is light weight and has good flexing. The better the rod, the more expensive they are which can mean several hundred dollars. However, it has been my experience that a fairly good eight foot graphite rod sells for less than $100 and will suffice for most avid fishermen. If you want the best, go to a tackle shop which usually handles the best, and they will recommend to you what is currently the most popular. Like high tech, there are constant improvements in fishing equipment.

Serious fly fishermen sometimes will fish all day, which entails constant strain on the angler's arms and wrists. Speaking from experience, the wrist especially can get tired, and could possibly develop carpel tunnel if worked hard and often enough. This is where the more expensive rods can be beneficial because they are very light weight, have the best flexing qualities, and are easy on the arm and wrist.

The length of the rod is usually 8 feet but some go to 8½ or 9 feet. I recommend that you do not get the lightest rod because sometimes, once the fly line gets wet it may be too heavy for the rod to cast normally. However, the light rod may be the best choice in small streams. This is why avid fly fishermen have more that one rig, and will choose which to use depending on where they are fishing and what flies they are using. Because rods come in different weights, it would be good to discuss with the fly shop what to use before purchasing one, and they will recommend the right rig for what you plan to do.

Recently there has been some anglers using the *spey* rod which is double handled, and comes longer than the regular fly rods. They are 11 to 14 feet in length which would seem to give them some advantage in the large rivers. Overall, however, I think the regular fly rod is better.

In the early years of trout fly fishing in the 20th century, the reels were of the automatic type. Some elderly fly fishermen, including myself, still use these reels. When you have been using something for decades, it is not easy to change. In my opinion, they are just as easy to use as the winding type; but since they are obsolete, we will focus on the winding type.

There are two types: the single-action and the multiplying reel. The single-action has 1 to 1 turning while the multiplying type, is geared up and turns faster than your hand turns. The single-action is, for most fishermen, good enough and is probably all that is used in southern Montana.

If one plans to fish often, it would be practical to get a quality reel that has smooth action and the feel of something solid. It should be big enough to hold at least 100 feet of line. The design should include a tension adjustment so that if a large fish is hooked, the tension should be set just strong enough to prevent the line from breaking. This allows for the fish to put up a fight and eventually tire out before the line breaks.

The fly line
There are different types of fly lines. The most common are the *weight-forward* line, which is heaviest toward the front or end of the line and the *double taper,* which is heaviest in the middle of the line and tapers down toward the ends.. The latter seems to be the most popular .

The double taper has some advantages when using dry flies because the thinner line at the end allows for more natural floating of the fly. Some like it because when one end of the line has deteriorated, such as losing floating characteristics, they just reverse the line in the reel and use the other end. Some fishermen have separate reels for each type of line, depending on whether they are dry or wet fly fishing, and the size of the stream.

Fly lines also have different floating characteristics. Some are designed to float the full length of the line while others have just front end sinking (sink tip). Probably most avid fly fishermen will have a sinking line on one reel for wet fly or bait fishing, while on another reel, a floating line for dry fly fishing.

There are different weights of lines: light weight (2-4), middle weight (5-7), and higher weights, which are more intended for salmon fishing. The best all around weight is 5-7 which is most commonly used and is recommended for beginners. Again if one is going to be a heavyweight trout fisherman, it is best to pay for a quality line. More could be said about lines, but one needs to get his feet wet before he can really decide what he prefers to use.

Fly lines have different designations which will be on the package. An example is WF-5-F which means weight forward, weight 5, floating line. Beginners may want to try out the different lines to get a feel for when to use each one. It may be a little costly, but rewarding, in the long run.

Leader Line
Attached to the end of the fly line is a clear monofilament line to which the flies or bait hooks are attached. The better ones for dry fly fishing taper down in weight toward the end to allow for more natural action of the fly. Trout do not see the leader. When fly fishing it is normal to have two flies attached: the end fly and the dropper fly which is attached two to three feet from the end. Most anglers will have two different flies on line with his favorite on the end. Each fly will have its own tippit tied to it, that is, a short light weight leader about 8 inches long and slightly lighter in weight than the main leader.

In southern Montana, a typical leader, when using flies, will be about a six or eight pound test weight. The small leaders attached to the flies will be four or six pound. You can buy leaders or make them from a roll of line by cutting a piece about seven feet and tie loops on the end and about three feet back, to which you attach the fly's tippit. It is a good idea to have several on hand because of the possibility of losing them from snags or in trees behind you Also, have several of your favorite flies with leaders already tied to them..When out in the stream, it is a good idea to have things as handy as possible so you do not have to keep going back to shore.

The small leader that attaches to the fly is called the *tippet*. It is lighter than the main leader to allow more natural action of the fly on the water, and in case of a snag, breaks instead of the main leader. It is practical to put these on the flies before going fishing.

Flies
When discussing flies, it is assumed we are talking about imitation flies or tied flies. The decision, as to what flies to use, is one of the more complicated aspects of fly fishing for trout. There are hundreds of new flies coming out constantly, and many are excellent replicas of the live insect.

The question is, what fly to use and when? I have tried perhaps a hundred different flies in my 40 years of experience. One hardly has the opportunity to try them all and be able to determine which ones work. None-the-less, my favorites have been narrowed to a few flies, and I no longer try anything else. Other fishermen have a different set of favorite flies. It is frustrating sometimes to determine what the trout are going for, yet this really is what makes it challenging and exciting.

There are several categories of flies that are produced: dry flies, wet flies, nymphs, terrestrials, streamers, midges and some others . To see a fairly good cross-section of most tied flies available, you might reference the books *Flies, The Best One Thousand* by Stetzer or *Trout Flies of The West* by Schellenger and Leeson. Besides these, there are other books available having exclusively to do with flies.

Live *nymphs* are aquatic insects that thrive and develop in the stream. They are the larvae, and they usually are found on the bottom and underneath the rocks. Some consider any imitation fly that is fished wet is a nymph. Those who are using these flies, are said to be nymphing.

Live *terrestrials* are insects that develop on land such as grasshoppers, ants, etc. One replica of the grasshopper is the *joe's hopper*, which is my first choice of any type of imitation fly. I have used it spring, summer and fall with fairly good success. So if you want to put on a tried and proven fly, try this one.

I have not used *streamers* much because I just did not have enough success with them. However, there are many anglers who swear by them. They know how to use them by streaking them with just the right action   Streaking means steady jerking of the line with a slight pause in between. This supposedly replicates a moving minnow, or something similar, in the water. Usually, they are fished close to the bottom of the stream.

Midges

These insects basically represent the small flies that are common on the water much of the year. Nearly all season you see mosquitoes and gnats flying around the water. When the food supply in the water is scarce, as in the fall, the trout will turn to feeding from the surface, including the midges.

Dry Flies

Fishing for trout with dry flies is, in my opinion, the most exciting of all fishing, especially in streams. Sometimes trout will jump high into the air to grab a fly before it lands on the water, and, I must say, this really gets your adrenalin going! I have seen large trout in excess of five pounds, especially rainbows, do this during the hatch of the stone fly (salmon fly) usually in June.

Dry flies, as a rule, are smaller than the other flies and usually amount to a small midge. Early and late in the season, when the water is low, they are the primary source of food. The most effective fly is the one the trout happen to be feeding on, and the best time is usually late in the evening; and even after sundown, if there is a bright moon. The trout will usually feed again in early morning after "sleeping", if that is what they actually do to rest, and they are hungry again.

It is a challenge to keep dry flies from getting water logged and thus sink. To prevent this, there are substances available that can be used to treat the fly. One I have used for decades is a waxy salve called mucilin. You simply rub it between forefinger and thumb, and then rub into the fly. This helps to keep the fly floating, but will wear off after an hour or so, in which case you will need to reapply. There are some dry fly treatments available now into which the fly can be dipped to make it buoyant, and that work better. To facilitate keeping a fly dry, you can do so by whipping it back and forth several times without letting it touch the water.

As stated, there are hundreds of fly imitations produced by a number of companies. There are imitations of various mayflies, caddis flies and terrestrials. What to use is an ongoing question because there are expert fly tiers who are constantly coming up with ingenious replicas.

Wet Flies
These flies simply differ from the dry fly in that they are intended to sink They are more preferred when there is high, but clear, water. During high water, there is more food in the river and, for this reason, the trout feed below the surface.

In deep water, some trout prefer to be near the bottom, which is particularly true of the brown trout. The wet fly is cast into water above a deep hole and allowed to achieve depth before entering the hole. A split shot sinker can be tied near the end of the line to get quicker depth, but using a sinker can sometimes lead to a snag.

The more common wet flies are the aquatic nymphs. One live aquatic insect that is a favorite of trout is the stonefly nymph, which some call the *hellgrammite*. (According to the MFW&P the *hellgrammite* is not another name for the stone fly nymph.) The live nymphs are very plentiful in Montana streams during spring until late June, when they hatch out. Browns love them and will move large stones to get at them. Many excellent replicas have been made, but I prefer to simply use the live stone fly nymphs, which I believe make the best overall bait.

What To Use
The answer to this question to some extent depends on the river. For instance, the Big Horn and the Beaverhead Rivers are tail waters, that is, they come out of dams. Certain insects flourish in these streams, especially if the waters are affected by limestone. The *Sow Bug* fly is one of the best on the Big Horn River, while on mountain fed streams, a good all around fly is the *caddis emerger.*

The *caddis emerger* is a very popular fly in Montana. It replicates the caddis fly when it emerges from its shell, in which it has developed on the bottom of the river. A favorite dry fly is the *pale moring dun,* which can be a good choice during low water in the fall.

Some of the common proven flies are displayed in chapter 10. A good all around fly, in my opinion, is the *joe's hopper,* fished dry or wet. When streams are low in the fall, you get the best results fishing it dry. Some might think it would only be effective in late summer and fall, the season for hoppers, but I have had success with them year around. It is, of course, a replica of the grass hopper. There are various imitations of the grasshopper, but I prefer the *joe's hopper.* In the bigger rivers I use the larger replica.

It helps to ascertain what the trout are feeding on, and then try to replicate it as close as possible. This may entail a very small fly, as small as a size 22. It is also a good idea to talk to the fly shops as to what new flies seem to be working well. Something new in recent years are the *beadheads* which the merchants say work good. They are good for nymphing because they have some built-in weight.

See chapter 10 for a list of time tested flies. There are thousands of flies available with numerous new ones coming out, but this list contains what has proven to get results. Some very impressive looking flies are actually very ineffective

A good bet for choosing the right fly is to ask people working in a local fly shop in the area of the stream you plan to fish. They can tell you what is currently working, which changes with the seasons.

Bait Fishing

On streams during the high water season, late May to mid July, it is usually best to use live bait, but wet flies can be used too if the water is not too murky. Casting with live bait is entirely different from fly casting, due to having a sinker on the line. When using a fly rod, the bait is basically swung out into the water, rather than casting as done with flies. Fishing with live bait can be done with a fly rod, however, a spinning outfit works better in the larger rivers because you can get more distance. However, if the stream is small, the fly rod works as well.

Some like to have two hooks on the line about three feet apart. I prefer to have just one hook because my experience has been that you have less snags, and you seldom catch fish on the upper hook. Whereas there are different ideas as to where to put the sinker, or split shot, I put it about two feet from the hook. To avoid snags, a float can be used further up the line from the split shot to keep the bait from sliding along the bottom

The *stone fly* nymph is a favorite meal of trout, especially the brown trout. As mentioned, the brown trout works hard to get at them on the bottom of the river. In mid summer after the hatch, you can see the shells of the nymphs stuck to stones To get these live nymphs, it is best to go to a spot on the stream where the water is shallow and moving fairly fast over large stones.

Two people need to work together, one with a large screen in the water, and the other kicking the stones upstream from the screen. The nymphs will float into the screen so they can easily be picked up and put into a container. You want to just pick the larger ones, as trout more readily go for them. (If you are hungry, flip one into your mouth and swallow whole as they are 100 percent protein. Do not panic if it crawls around in your stomach. They do not bite!).

The next best bait is the grasshopper, particularly the large greenbacks that have the yellow belly. There have been times when I could only catch fish if I had a hopper on the line. If you can not get stone fly nymphs, then use grasshoppers if they are available. In early spring and after summer when the nights get cold, the hoppers are hard to get, but the best bait to use at these time are flies anyway.

The bait that is always available is worms. If you can not get them yourself by digging for them, you can always buy them at a sporting goods store or convenience store in the vicinity of the fishing. The best worms are the nightcrawlers. You fish them the same as other bait. They seem to be the best bait when still fishing in lakes.

There are other types of bait which are sometimes effective: corn, fish eggs, fish meat, power bait, even marshmallow. Some people have reported that baby shrimp are good bait. These types of bait are usually used in lakes or in large holes on the bigger rivers.

Spin Fishing
Although I prefer fly fishing, sometimes conditions dictate that the best catch is had by using lures. The equipment includes a spinning rod and reel with about 80

yards of clear monofilament line. Depending on the size of the stream, you need to choose what weight of line to use. A good all around weight is 8 pound. In the smaller streams, you can get by with lighter weight line, but you might as well keep the 8 pound test line.

Again, if one plans to do extensive fishing, it is best to get quality equipment. There is a wide range of reels with different price tags. There are small spinning reels, but these are not nearly as good as the larger ones when fishing rivers of any size. I do not recommend the small spinning reels. The good reels will have tension control, which becomes necessary when hooking a large fish that can put several pounds of pull on the line. By simply trying the reel, you can get a feel for the gear and bearing action. You should be able to switch the handle to left or right side depending on whether you are left or right handed. Check the bail to see that it clicks open and shut with firmness. The rods are usually five or six feet long and do not need to be made of graphite. A good fiberglass rod will do the job and is much cheaper.

Like fly fishing, there is a large choice of lures to use. My first choice is the *thomas cyclone,* simply because it has produced the most strikes. Next in line is the *hammered brass daredevil* and the *mepps.* There are hundreds of different lures with all kinds of fancy colors and odd shapes available but most of these are a waste of money. Some are using the *panthur martin,* of which there are several variations, with good results. These look somewhat like the *mepps.* There is some indication that trout do not necessarily go after lures for food. Some say the trout are fighting an intruder, and they are especially sensitive during spawning. Thus, this may be a case for using lures when the trout are spawning.

POPULAR LURES left to right: Panthur Martins, Hammerd Brass, Thomas Cyclone

Waders or hip boots

When trout fishing, there is a need to wade out into the water for various reasons. You may need to get away from the bank because of heavy brush that inhibits getting any distance when casting. Especially during fly fishing, one moves around in the stream and sometimes gets into water chest high. It is more popular to use waders which come up high on the chest allowing for deep wading. The current waders available have become much lighter, but also more expensive; however, they are worth the money. Along with the waders, you need to get heavy duty shoes with felt soles to prevent slipping on the rocks. In some states felt soles have been outlawed, but not so in Montana, as of 2012.

Hip boots are preferred by some, but have really become outdated. Boots can, at times, allow for water to get in if not careful when wading in thigh-high water. So, the recommended equipment is waders. As an alternative for younger anglers, a pair of tennis shoes and levis works good. All the years of my growing up and into my 40's, I preferred this; and it did not bother me to get wet clear up to the waist. I would go back to boots during the times the water was especially cold, in early spring and fall; but on the hot summer days, it was a cool and refreshing way to go. To get dry at the end of fishing, you just change clothes.

When purchasing waders, it is a good idea to get quality stuff that does not easily tear. Be sure to get the size that fits best, and the footing is the right size. If the footing is too big, your feet may experience irritation

Other Accessories

Creel

There are all kinds of fishing bags - be sure to get one large enough to carry several trout, twelve inches or better. In my early years, most anglers used the woven reed type creel. I prefer these over the canvas bag because you can stuff them with heavy grass along with the fish you catch, and this keeps the fish colder and less likely to spoil before getting them into ice. Like so many good things, they have become obsolete; but they are coming some back. You can sometimes find them in antique shops, but be prepared to pay at least $50 for one.

Fishing Vest

This accessory is hard to be without, especially for fly fishermen. You need somewhere to put all the paraphernalia needed to do fly fishing: boxes of flies, sinkers, leaders, dry fly liquid, pliers, knife, spinners, swivels (for attaching spinners during spin fishing), etc.

Net

This is one piece of equipment that is not always necessary, but it is a good idea to have one with you. If you are in the middle of the stream and need to land a fish, to do so without a net is difficult, especially if the fish is of any size. Nets can be had for less than $20, and it really is practical to have one with you. Arrange it so it hangs behind your back, so when walking through brush, it does not get caught on twigs.

Fly Caddie

These little boxes are designed to keep your flies orderly. They come with a foam bottom to hook them into so you can easily extract them. Avid anglers have more than one to keep the different kinds of flies separate: wet flies, nymphs, dry flies, streamers. They come with a snap that allows for hanging them on your vest, or they can simply be kept in a pocket. Some have compartments to allow for keeping the flies separate and having the tippit already tied on.

Strike Indicator

Small device that is brightly colored and floats attached near the end of the fly line to reveal when a strike is taking place. At times, it may be helpful in setting the hook.

Clothing

It is best to wear clothing with earth tone colors that blend more with the background. Avoid bright colors. Trout can be spooked if they see you; however, they do not have good vision at a low angle to the water surface. In other words, you need to be somewhat close for them to see you. It makes good sense to have extra clothing to handle unexpected cold. Your pants should be somewhat heavy, like levis, to handle pokes and scrapes you get walking through brush.

Keep wallet and check book safe

Leave your wallet and check book hidden in your vehicle because you never know when you might slip or stumble and fall into the water.

Hat, sunglasses

Most fishermen prefer them some kind of head cover to keep direct sun off the head, and some hook flies to their hat. A popular hat that keeps the sun off and sheds rain is the *Tilly Hat*. Along with a good hat, one needs to have a good pair of sun glasses, especially ones that block ultraviolet rays and are polarized, which reduces glare off the water. The polarized glasses enable the angler to see into the water better, besides making it easier on the eyes.

Rain Jacket
There are times when one wants to keep fishing even though it is raining. Therefor, a good rain jacket should be kept on hand just in case.

Spinners
A good supply of these is needed, if spin fishing, because there is a tendency to lose them to snags in the water. Keep several different types in your chest caddie, described below. Also, when spin fishing, you need a lot of *swivels* that are used to attach the spinner to the line.

Chest Caddie
A device that is very handy, especially when out in the water, is a small plastic box with compartments in it to hold flies, sinkers or other items. It hangs from the neck and has a strap that goes around the abdomen to hold it close. A flap folds down and provides a little platform to facilitate little tasks that need to be done; such as attaching sinkers, leaders, swivels, etc.

Pliers, Wire Cutters, Knife
A needle-nose pliers is needed to remove hooks from deep in the throat of fish just landed, and squeezing split shot onto leaders.. Wire cutters are helpful for cutting lines. A good sharp knife is needed for many things, including cleaning the fish. A multiple use knife, like the *Swiss Army Knife,* is very handy to have.

Split shot (small sinkers)
These items can be purchased in handy little plastic dispensers that contain a variety of sizes and are made for easy dispensing. They usually come with a snap that allows for hanging on the vest, and can easily be detached. Depending on the water flow volume and the depth of the stream, a variety of split shot are required. For deep holes, a size pss 4 split shot would probably work best. Smaller holes would call for a pss 5 or 7. In fast moving current, the large size may be needed to get the bait or nymph deeper more quickly.

Bait Hooks
These come is various sizes; basically 4,6 and 8. The larger the number, the smaller the hook.. When using bait in a small stream where the fish are 10 inches

or under, use a size 8 hook. In larger streams, use a 4 or 6. Large grasshoppers usually require a 4.

Live Bait Caddie
When live bait fishing, it is handy to have a belt caddie to hold the bait. They are designed for easy access. When using grasshoppers, you want to squeeze their heads before putting them into the caddie. This will somewhat immobilize them so they do not jump out when you are opening the lid.

Mosquito spray and Sun Block
These should be included as necessary supplies when going fishing. Mosquitoes can take the joy out of a trip if you do not have a repellant. Sun block is highly recommended by health authorities to prevent skin cancer.

Bear spray
Encounters with bears are somewhat rare, but there is always the possibility for one. Even if encountered, there is usually no danger, unless it is a sow with cubs. In the case of an attack, the spray is effective when directed at the face. Some feel that the only sure thing is a pistol, at least 44 caliber.

Montana Fishing Regulations
This publication from the MFW&P, provides necessary information about the streams and lakes as to times of year fishing is allowed, limits of fish, whether catch and release, and other regulations.. A fishing license must be procured before going fishing, and when doing so, a copy of this publication can be obtained, free of cost. Senior citizens get by for minimal cost Out-of-state anglers pay a substantial fee, which can cover a couple days or for all season.

Montana Atlas and Gazetteer
This publication, available in fly shops and other stores, provides topographical maps for all areas of the state. Included are charts that show what species of trout are found in the main streams and lakes, the different state and federal lands and parks having fishing accesses, and campgrounds.

CHAPTER 7

TROUT FISHING TECHNIQUE

TROUT FISHING TECHNIQUE

To be effective at trout fishing, it is important to have the right equipment, as discussed in the previous chapter. It is also important to have the right technique.

FLY FISHING
Casting
Fly casting technique is done differently in different types of situations: such as the size of the stream, high or low water, brush along the bank, wet or dry fly, and nymph fishing. When fishing a river of any size, one needs to know how to get distance with the line. A new angler will need to practice in his back yard or any big open area before going to the stream.

You begin by casting the line forward then thrusting the line back behind you and repeating, letting out a little line each time, keeping the line high enough from hitting the ground. As the length of line out gets long, it takes some practice to learn exactly when to thrust the line forward. Simply put, the line needs to be completely stretched out behind you at the time you cast forward. If done too early, the cast forward will only take up slack, and the line will simply fall to the ground or hit you in the back So, you need to practice casting until you get a feel for the timing. When you are out on the stream, it will be necessary to have open space behind you to do distance casting. This may require wading out away from the shore..

Casting flies with brush at your back requires a different type of casting. There are a couple of ways to send your line out into the water. One way is to use rolling action. This method entails rolling your line and directing the line straight away from you after it has stretched out somewhat downstream. Of course, this will not work if too much line is out. Or you can whip your line back and forth across the front of you, and then, at a certain point, send the line forward. Not much distance can be achieved by either method. An alternative would be to use a spinning outfit, and cast the fly out with a float attached. This, of course, would enable you to get greater distance.

Another method of casting is the *roll cast,* which is different from that described in the previous paragraph.   There are times when this is the best method to use, depending on brush and other factors. It will become apparent when to do this as you gain experience. You should have a good double taper float line and a graphite rod with good flexing. The method was pretty well described in the book: The

Dorling Kindersley Encyclopedia of Fishing:

> Begin by taking a suitable stance, with one foot slightly in front of the other and the rod pointing down the line. Then begin a smooth, steady draw, raising your rod hand to just above shoulder height and lifting the rod to 10:30 or 11:00 position. This steady draw allows a loop of line to form between the rod top and the water. While the line is still moving, raise the rod slightly, then punch it rapidly forward and down. The rod is now flexed and under maximum compression, and the line follows its path, bellying out slightly behind you and coming off the water close to your feet. As you power the rod down through the 3:00 position, the belly of the line will roll forward. Follow through smoothly so that the line unfolds and straightens above the water.

Another method is to send your line forward by pulling it back, as you would with bow and arrow, and then letting go. Not much distance can be achieved this way, but in some situations, it may be the only way. When using wet flies, you can put a small split shot near the end of the leader and basically swing the line out into the water. You can eventually get the knack of it by doing it.

Using Dry Flies

As stated in the previous chapter, you will need the proper fly line, a weight forward or a double taper line.. The benefits of each is discussed in the chapter *Trout Fishing Equipment and Accessories.* One needs to learn how to manipulate the fly on the water so as to get as much naturalness as possible.

The angler needs to know where in the water to put the fly. How to read the water to ascertain where the fish might be lying, is discussed in chapter 12. When casting into the type of water where fish reside, I usually drop a dry fly directly onto the spot. This requires skill in casting. If done with accuracy it can get the most strikes. If this does not work, then you should cast the fly above the spot so that it floats naturally on the surface into the area. I am somewhat impatient, and so I will move on if I do not get a strike after several casts

As you gain experience, you learn how to place the fly and how to manipulate it. The objective is to achieve naturalness, or you might say, get the fly to imitate the live fly's habits on the water. Trout seem to have some ability to distinguish between what is real and what is fake.

When dry fly fishing, do not let your line continue to float down stream eventually laying in the water completely stretched out. Doing so is a waste of time. Your fly should only be out from you for a matter of a few seconds before whipping it backward and then out again. This is the essence of dry fly fishing: you want your fly primarily in the area of the water that has the most promise.

If the stretch of water, or hole, you are fishing is relatively small surrounded by fast water, aim your fly to land directly on the hole. This is especially important if the main trout in the area is the rainbow. Rainbows often times will go for your fly before it hits the water. A brown trout feeding off the surface will hit it at the time it lands

To some extent I have over simplified the techniques involved. My intention is to give a novice a good grasp of the basics. .

May Fly, Salmon Fly, and Caddis Hatch

Sometime in May or June, or slightly earlier, most rivers will have the may fly or stone fly hatch take place. The caddis hatch is usually about mid May, so some call it, the "Mother's Day hatch". Hatches begin in the lower stretches of the river where the water is warmer and slowly move up the river. The adult fly emerges from the nymph, and either sits on or flies along the surface. The river gets covered with them. The trout will go into a wild eating frenzy and gorge themselves.

If you find yourself in the middle of a hatch, put a replica of the fly on your line. Usually, you can get your limit of trout very quickly. Most experienced anglers will tell you this is an exciting time to be on the river because the fishing is sensational. You will see some trout jumping clear out of the water to get a fly. May fly hatches occur for most of the warmer months. These aquatic flies are the most popular and frequently used during the year.

Wet Flies

Wet fly nymphing or live bait fishing in streams is usually done when there is high water. This action is called *drift fishing*, which means you are allowing your fly or bait to move with the current and sometimes weighted to give it more depth. Basically, you cast somewhat upstream and let the fly go with the flow. Then when stretched out down stream, you cast it back upstream again.

The technique involved with wet flies is, in many respects, similar to dry flies. It just does not require the finesse. You do not have to go to the trouble of placing the fly just right, keeping the fly dry, and working a small area in the stream. Whatever spot you are fishing, you simply cast the fly above it and let it sink and flow into it. Depending on how big the stream is and how deep the hole, you may want to put a split shot sinker near the end of the leader. Many veteran fly fishermen prefer no sinker so they can cast as you would with dry flies.

Caddisflies and Midges

These are two other types of insects where the larvae develop on the bottom of the stream. When the time comes for them to hatch, they rise to the surface and the adult emerges from the larvae. Replicas of these flies are quite smaller than the stone fly or May fly but, at times, get better results.

Nymph Fishing

Over all, the majority of the food of the trout are *nymphs*, that is, the larva of aquatic insects, some of which have more than one stage of development. They develop on the bottom of rivers and are present for much of the year. The stone fly larva exists more in the spring and early summer, but a replica of it can be effective all year. Fishing with flies that replicate the nymphs is referred to as *nymphing*. Drift fishing, usually with a small splitshot, is the technique used

The nymph flies are designed to replicate the premature stage of an insect, which can be any of the following: stone flies, may flies, caddisflies, dragonflies, and damselflies. The body of the fly is thickest at the front and tapers to the back with fibers tied in to look like legs. Sometimes anglers make the mistake of using a fly too large. It is best not only to use a fly that matches the shape of the nymph, but also its size.

When trout are feeding on nymphs, at times they are going after certain ones beneath the surface, in which case you will see bulges in the water. You should put on a fly that replicates what they are eating as exactly as possible in size and shape. You can determine this by pumping the stomach of your first fish to see what they are actually eating. Also, you will find it helpful to have a strike indicator on your line. If the water is deep and moving somewhat fast, a splitshot may also be needed.

Live bait fishing

When fishing streams, my first choice is the a large stone fly nymph, followed by the large grasshopper, then worms. It is necessary to have the line weighted some by a small split shot in order to cast and get some distance out into the water. The size of the split shot depends on how fast and how deep the water is. You should have a supply of various size split shots, which is the way they are packaged. You may change the amount of weight, depending on the hole you are fishing. As mentioned a number of times, this whole method needs to be learned mainly by doing it.

Casting is a matter of just swinging the line out, somewhat upstream, if using a fly rod, which is usually what is best in small streams. In larger streams, the best method is the spinning outfit with float and split shot near the bait. Depending on the size of the stream, you place the float a couple feet from the bait. About 10 inches from the bait, you place a small split shot. This method allows for fishing long distances from shore and keeps the bait sufficiently below the surface.

During High Water
About mid-May the spring runoff begins which brings high murky water. This is the best time to fish with live bait or spinners. At this time, the fish are found closer to the bank because the water is not so fast, and that is where most of the insects and other food are found. In this case, the way to fish is just use a small sinker and cast the bait close to the bank, and allow it to drift into these holes.

Spin Fishing
Although fly fishing is the most fun, sometimes various factors dictate using a spinning outfit. For example, in the larger streams during high water, fly fishing is usually not practical. Or sometimes one just simply wants a little variety, or be able to reach holes not in range of a fly outfit.

Fishing with lures entails casting the lure out some distance and reeling it back at an appropriate rate, depending on whether the lure is in fast or slow water. It is best to reel it so that the lure replicates a minnow moving through the water, rather than fast spinning. However, some lures such as the *Mepps* are made to spin Consequently, in fast water you wind slowly, and in slow water, wind more rapidly to avoid snagging on the bottom. How to cast a spinning outfit can be demonstrated by the clerk at the store where you buy it. He will show you how to grasp the line with the forefinger, set the bail, and when to let go as you cast.

To become adept at spin casting, a novice should practice in a large field or in the back yard. Put a lure, without the hook, on the end of your line and cast at targets various distances away. When you can drop the lure consistently within two or three feet of the target, perhaps a small bucket, at a distance of 25 yards or more, you will be much better equipped to reach areas where there are fish hard to reach. For example, there may be a large boulder a long distance out in the stream, and you want to drop the lure right behind it. This is sometimes desirable because if there is a trout there, the sudden splash may startle him and induce him to strike. Or you may want to cast just beyond and upstream of the boulder, and then reel the lure through the hole. Whatever the case, one may want to drop the lure in a certain spot. This takes some ability.

A beginner will want to practice casting overhand and sideways. This ability is needed because the brush behind you on the stream may dictate one or the other. Stream fishing for trout often involves navigating difficult terrain, such as a lot of brush at your back, a steep sloping bank or other obstacles.

Any of the lures mentioned in the chapter on equipment can be productive. My favorites are the *Thomas Cyclone*, the *hammered brass daredevil,* and the *Panthur Martin*. In the large streams, it is recommended to use an *open bail spinning reel* because they give you the ability to cast the furthest If you want to reach a greater distance, you can do so with a heavier lure. There are some lures that are made from thicker metal stock and thus are heavier. I like using them on the Yellowstone River because it is wider then the other rivers. However, these heavy lures seem to be getting harder to find.

The question is, Where do you cast the lure? When fishing a large deep hole, cast the lure upstream somewhat so the lure has time to gain some depth. In a large stream with boulders in the water, you cast out and somewhat upstream of a boulder, and then reel the lure through the hole behind the boulder. To become really adept at this, will take some experience over time.

It is possible to spin fish with flies. This is done by using a float tied to your line about 4 feet back from the fly. If using a wet fly, add a splitshot about one foot from the fly, which will put it well below the surface. The same would be true if using live bait. Cast out and upstream and then let it drift back downstream. Place the bait at different spots and try to work the whole area.

Still fishing

This is the type of fishing done in lakes and large holes in a river. Some prefer this type of fishing because it requires little effort, and enables companions to relax in a folding chair on the bank and enjoy conversation. It amounts to casting out your bait with a sinker by it and having it sit on the bottom of the stream or lake. You just sit and wait for the fish to strike. Or, some like to use a split shot near the bait with a float further up. After casting out, you watch the float which will submerge when a fish strikes. The spinning outfit works very well because it enables you to get the most distance.

Lake Fishing

Fly Fishing

Fishing with flies on a lake can be fun when the fish are feeding from the surface. You can sometimes see a good size trout breaking the surface. If it is in range of your casting, try to drop your fly precisely where it is feeding. The fly you use should be a replica of what the fish are feeding on or use something as close as possible.

An enjoyable way to fly fish on a lake is to use a float tube. This device has an inflatable tube that goes around the waist and keeps you afloat so you can go out into the lake, giving you a much larger area to fish. Of course, a boat can be used also.

At times, the best time to fly fish is late evening, or even after sundown when there is a bright moon. This can be the best time because there are more insects on the water. If there is a stream flowing into the lake, this may be the best place to catch fish. The trout may tend to hang out there because this is where food may be entering the lake.

You can fish the lake using a spinning outfit and lures or use bait and still fish. Sometimes during the heat of day, you may find this more relaxing to get out of the direct sunlight and sit under an umbrella with your line out.

Some prefer to fish lakes in a boat, which allows you to cover more territory. You can move slowly along the shore, say 50 to 100 yards out, and cast toward shore using flies or lures.

Fishing in high mountain lakes requires some advanced familiarity with the lakes you are headed for. Some of these lakes produce fish only at certain times and using specific bait. A long hike could lead to disappointment if the lake is still frozen or you do not have the right bait. Fly shops in the region can usually instruct you on when to go and what to use. Or, if the pocketbook allows, you can sign up with an outfitter to guide you into the high mountain areas. He may even provide horseback if you prefer that.

Trolling

Probably the most popular way to fish on lakes is by trolling. What anglers usually use are *cowbells* which consists of a series of shiny spinners in a row on a leader, and with a minnow or worm on the end. There is other colorful, flashy stuff available that can be added to the line for the purpose of attracting the trout, and apparently this has some success.

The line is let out to 50 feet or more and dragged behind the boat as it moves over the water. The boat is equipped with a trolling motor that allows for very slow movment through the water. The anglers can just sit back, enjoy refreshment, conversation, and wait for a strike.

Fishing in The Rain
Some anglers will stop fishing when it starts raining, but sometimes that is when one can have the best fishing. On numerous occasions, I have had good success in rain storms using wet flies or bait. So, it is a good idea to keep a rain jacket on hand.

CHAPTER 8
TROUT FOOD

What trout feed on depends on a number of factors such as time of year, volume of water flow, food available in the stream at any one time, and size of the fish. There are times when food becomes scarce for them, which happens late in the fall when the streams are low. It is helpful for anglers to have some knowledge of the insects (the larvae and adult stage) they are feeding on because this determines what fly to use. The following is a list of the various aquatic, terrestrial insects and other types of food that appear at different times of the year.

Stonefly
This aquatic insect begins its development on the bottom of the stream. As the larvae grows it can be found under rocks and sometimes moving across the bottom making it an easy target for a hungry trout. When full grown it can be one to two inches in length and is 100% protein. The trout, especially the browns, love them. In fact, they seem to be the preferred food over everything else.

When it reaches maturity, it crawls out of the water onto a rock or other surface and hatches into the stonefly, also known as the salmon fly. It leaves its shell behind, and these shells can be seen on practically every rock. This hatch takes place in late May or early June, but the exact time varies with each stream. It starts in the warmer waters down stream and slowly moves upstream, and one quickly becomes aware he is in the middle of it by the abundance of stoneflies everywhere. The trout go crazy for them, jumping out of the water sometimes to get one flying close to the surface. Even big trout will clear the water sometimes as much as three or four feet. It really is an exciting moment if one is fortunate enough to be there when it happens.

The best place to find them is in somewhat fast moving shallow water that has lots of large stones. You can harvest them by using a large screen, holding it down in the water, and having someone else kick the rocks just upstream, which will dislodge them so that they drift into the screen. These larvae seem to be the best bait you can use, that is, if they are available.

Mayfly
Like the stonefly, the mayfly nymph develops on the bottom of the stream The nymph stage lasts most of the life of the insect, which can be up to a year, and

looks like a smaller version of the stone fly larvae. It also hangs out under rocks and so the trout will move the rocks to get to them. When it reaches maturity, it swims to the surface and hatches into a *dun* or *subimago*. This is the first stage of adulthood. At this point, it floats on the water to allow its wings to dry, an easy prey for the trout. After a very short time, it flies to vegetation along the stream where it emerges as a *spinner*, the fully developed adult. It is identifiable by its two large wings and two long tail filaments.

The mayfly hatches in the spring and fall; and when they do, the trout have a feast. The logical choice for a fly to put on your line, at this time, would be a replica of it.

Caddisfly
This is perhaps the hardiest of aquatic insects in the streams. There are two stages to its lifet, the larva and the pupa. The wormlike larvae is cream colored with a dark head. It makes a casing to live in while it develops. This is made from a secreted substance combined with sand and other material, and can be seen attached to rocks. At times, the case can be seen being pulled along on the bottom by the larvae. Trout will often have a belly full of these insects, including casings.

After a year, the larvae seal themselves in their casing and develop wings and legs. Then after a few more weeks they emerge and head for the surface where they fly away as an full adult   As with the mayfly, they are the most vulnerable when they swim to the surface.

A recommended fly to use is one that replicates the larvae which trout relish more than the winged adult.

Midges
This is the smallest of the aquatic insects, and it also has two stages of development, the larvae and pupa. The larvae is thinner than the caddisfly larvae. They are found in various places in the water: in sand, mud and on leaves or twigs. Trout have an appetite for them, more so than the adult.

If the trout are feeding on the airborne adults after a hatch, you might get some strikes using an imitation.. The fly is very small, in the range of a mosquito. If the exact fly is not available, use one that is small and dark and may draw the trout anyway. You may need to use a very small fly, possibly a size 22.

Crane Fly

This is a large insect that looks like the granddaddy of mosquitoes. It has the same shape as the mosquitoe, but is much larger. The larvae has shape of a small caterpillar. These insects exist in some streams, such as the Beaverhead; and like the stonefly, the trout love them.

Grasshopper

In some years there is an abundance of grasshoppers; and in other years not so many. However, this terrestrial insect is an excellent live bait for catching trout. The best hopper to use is what we call the greentop. It is the largest and easiest to see in the water, having a yellow belly along with the green top.

Sometimes, when you are out in the grass to catch them in the early cool morning, you can find them by getting down and spreading the grass, as they will stay there until it warms up. After catching one, squeeze its head, which will somewhat immobilize it, and make it easier to stuff into your bait can. Then when you open the bait can to get one, they are less likely jump out. The best all around imitation fly to use in catching trout is the *Joe's hopper*.

Worms

When the water is high like at runoff stage, worms can get swept off of banks into the water. So they are trout food to some extent, but not nearly as much as the aquatic insects. They seem to be the best when still fishing from shore in the lakes, using a bobber and splitshot.

Minnows

As trout get large, they tend to feed on larger sources of food, one being the minnow, but seldom do you find them in trout under three pounds. Some trout, such as the dolly varden, have more of a tendency to feed on them.

There are tied flies that replicate the minnow, usually in the form of a streamer, and some have good success with them. There are also lures that replicate the minnow.

At one time, a special rig for using live minnows for bait was called a *gang hook*. This rig consists of a sawed off nail which is slid into the mouth of the minnow to which are attached two tippits with three-prong hooks that hang beside the minnow. It is cast out using a spinning outfit. Some anglers still use it today. (Anyone using minnows are strongly cautioned not to throw the left over minnows into the stream or lake. In fact, there may soon, if not already, be a stiff fine for

doing it.)
Crawfish
These are crustaceans that inhabit the bottom of some streams. They are found in the lower Madison river and contribute to the rapid growth of the trout, but not many streams have them.

Sculpins
Small bullhead type creature that is a resident in some streams. Trout go for them.

Frogs, mice
These are found only in the larger trout, likely over three pounds. There are lures that replicate them, but it has been my experience that they do not work very well.

Other miscellaneous
Of course there are other types of food such as; ants, beetles, bees, wasps, wooly worms and other insects, all of which will be eaten by trout. However, these are not as popular with the trout as the aquatic insects. There are also tied flies that imitate them, but it seems to be a wasted effort to use them.

CHAPTER 9
FISHING DURING THE DIFFERENT SEASONS

Out of state visitors hoping to do some trout fishing should be aware of the effect the different seasons have on the fishing. During the period of about October 15 to March 15, the weather is usually too cold to enjoy it; and much of the water may be frozen over.

In the Winter, some rivers such as the Big Horn and the Beaverhead, which come out of dams, have enough warmth in the water to keep from freezing; and there can be fairly good fishing at this time. They are not fished as heavy as the rest of the year, and there are days when the weather is not so cold.

Perhaps the most undesirable times to fish are the winter months and sometimes in mid summer. It can get fairly hot in July and August, which can take some of the enjoyment out of it, not to speak of being annoyed by mosquitos and other pests. Also, from around late May until mid July, the streams have their run off, and the water is too high and can be very murky. This is not a good time to fly fish, but you can still get some fish using bait, usually close to shore, where the trout are more likely to hang out because the main stream is high and moving fast.

Some like to fish the rivers during runoff using lures, which can get some good results. A good lure to use at this time, would be one with bright color such as a hammered brass.

It is not recommended to float the larger rivers during runoff because it can be dangerous. None the less, it is still done; but it is a good idea to have an experienced guide along, one who knows the river.

So, the most desirable times to fish would be March to late May and late July to mid October. However, if the streams are not good at this time, then it might be a good time to try the lakes.

Fly fishing is the best when the water is not high. There are different hatches that take place during the year, as can be seen in chapter 10. When these hatches are taking place, it is best to put on a replica of the fly that is emerging.

Dry fly fishing, a favorite of many, is mostly done after the runoff when the river has come down, and there are more flies on the water and less food under the surface. Rainbows are more frequently caught during this time.

CHAPTER 10
POPULAR TIED FLIES

There are hundreds of different flies available but this is a list of time-tested flies that have proven to be successful in getting fish. Some are good for all year round, while others are more seasonal and related to the corresponding fly hatch. The Big Horn River and Beaverhead River are tailwaters which makes for more constant water temperature, and they also have limestone minerals which creates an environment that produces large trout. The types of flies that are affective in these rivers are different than those for other streams.

When a particular hatch is taking place, anglers need to take note and try a fly that replicates what is hatching. This is what is called "match the hatch". Ordinarily, this is the fly to use, but not necessarily the only one. To find out what the fish are truly feeding on, it can be revealing to pump the stomach.

On the Big Horn River, the following flies are recommended according to the seasonal hatches:

midges	March - May
blue wing olive (BWO)	April to October
pale morning dun (PMD)	July - September
black or tan Caddis	July - September
trico	August - October
yellow sallies	June - August

A fully equipped and prepared angler would most likely carry a supply of the following flies that seem to be the most successful, according to a consensus:

Photos contributed by *Catch Fly Fishing LLC*

NYPMPHS - YEAR AROUND

SCUD - ORANGE OR PINK

SAN JUAN WORM

STREAMERS

WOLLEY BUGGER

MUDDLER

TERRESTRIALS - YEAR AROUND

JOE'S HOPPER

MORRISH HOPPER

ERIK'S CLODHOPPER

NYPMPHS - YEAR AROUND

CADDIS EMERGER

SOWBUG IN SOFT HACKLE

HARE'S EAR

PHEASANT TAIL

DRY FLIES (primarily spring and fall)

ADAMS

BLACK GNAT

DRY FLIES (primarily spring and fall)

PALE MORING DUN (PMD)

BLUE WING OLIVE (BWO)

STONE FLY HATCH

SOFA PILLOW

CHAPTER 11
FLY TYING

Some fishermen have discovered an enjoyable hobby - tying their own flies. This hobby has a two fold benefit. First, it allows one to be creative in trying to replicate live aquatic or terrestrial flies that are natural to his area. Second, there is the somewhat minor matter, that of saving money.

What makes it especially enjoyable is the challenge of coming up with something new and then putting it to the test. However, one has to be able to handle very small work which can be taxing. Those who do take it up, seem to enjoy it very much.

To get started, there are kits available that have the tools and all kinds of material to make the flies. Pay a visit to a fly shop where you can get the kits and also some good advice on how to do it. As you get adept at it, you will probably advance to more exotic creations.

There are some who have made a name for themselves tying flies. Whereas most fly shops purchase their flies from various commercial sources, the Big Horn Fly and Tackle Shop in Billings has the expertise to tie many of the ones they sell. They can be very helpful getting you started.

CHAPTER 12
READING THE WATER

This chapter has to do with observing the stream and perceiving where the trout are likely to be in the water. There are certain factors that affect this: depth of water, rate of flow, cover, and areas that produce food. This may seem simple to figure out, but the truth of the matter is, it takes a skilled angler to have a good grasp on this. Where the trout are hanging out, is not always so obvious, requiring experience and a trained eye.

The most obvious type of water that attracts trout is deep, slow moving water which is, of course, commonly referred to as a "hole". In fact, any type of water that the trout seek, fishermen refer to as a hole. Deep slow moving water is where you most often find the larger fish. To many anglers, this is the more obvious place to fish. Even more attractive, is deep water under a ripple. Ripples usually are caused by fast moving shallow water flowing into deep water. It seems rainbow trout especially seek this type.

The problem with the obvious deep holes is that they get fished the most. In streams that are heavily fished, most anglers usually just fish the deep holes and often just sit and still fish with bait and sinker. Experienced anglers, for this reason, spend little time in them and move onto the less obvious holes, which may actually contain more fish.

Another type of water is the area behind boulders. These types of holes are, in some cases, called "pocket holes" referring to the slow swirling water behind the boulder. Trout hang out here, rather than out in the fast moving current, because it does not require effort to hold a steady position. This is true of the brown trout when compared to the rainbow. They like these holes for another reason , that is, it is convenient for feeding because they can watch the fast water moving past that brings the food. Novice anglers do not realize also, that immediately ahead of a boulder there are eddies that trout may be in, and they may pass up these spots. Even at the base of a waterfall in the plunge pool, there can be an eddy that cycles through a recess under the wall. In some cases, trout will be present there.

You might think that fast water, even white water, would not hold any fish, but it is a fact that sometimes rainbow trout are caught there. Browns seldom are caught in this type of water, perhaps because they are not as energetic or maybe do not need the high oxygen in the water that rainbows seem to like.

Another type of water to look for, is an undercut along a bank, where it is somewhat deep and moving at a moderate pace. This type of water is also often passed over by inexperienced anglers. It is even more likely not fished when it is on the opposite side of the stream. There is an area of the Stillwater River at Castle Rock Campground that has this feature. The big attraction at the campground is a beautiful deep hole that runs for about a hundred yards, and the fishermen favor it. However, just downstream there is a shallow sandbar in the middle of the river that is about the same length. Against the opposite bank is a long deep hole with moderate moving water. There is a way to get out to the sandbar and from there, cast flies into the hole against the opposite bank. It requires the capability to cast long distance to reach it with a fly outfit. Not having the brush immediately behind you, makes it possible to reach, but not likely for a novice. This water has often produced several nice browns.

When the trout are feeding on mayflies, for example, you can tell where they are in the water by watching where they rise. This will give you somewhat of an indication of where they like to hang out. The best time to observe this is sometimes during twilight with a bright moon.

Trout also like to hang out under overhanging limbs or brush in the water which provides cover they seem to like. The browns especially seem to prefer shade. The danger of fishing this type of hole is that it is easy to get your line snagged. The best bet is to use a wet fly or bait with sinker, and allow the bait to pass close to it. Sometimes the trout will dash out to get it.

Overall, it is best to go to an area that is not heavily fished. One way you can do this, is by going to a rancher or farmer and asking permission to fish on his land. From past experience, most of the time they will consent. If he consents, be sure to show respect for his place by not doing careless things, such as leaving gates open. According to Montana Fish and Game laws, you can fish anywhere on any stream as long as you are below the high water line. As of this date, however, there are land owners who are challenging this law.

When spin fishing on one of the larger rivers, it is best to cast into holes near the opposite bank, as these are not fished as much. By doing this, you might be surprised at what you catch - some very large trout. It is best to cast to a deep hole and land your lure into the middle of it. This may startle a trout, and, being territorial, he may quickly attack it.

As a general rule, one side of a stream is fished harder, which is the one on the same side as the access road or the campground if one is present. For this reason, there will be more fish present and less spooked on the opposite side. If you cannot reach the other side with flies, switch to a spinning outfit. You may be surprised at the results, even though the area is said to be "fished out".

More could be said about where to fish in a stream. Again, it is a skill that comes with experience, but what has been written here, will certainly help.

CHAPTER 13
GUEST RANCHES, OUTFITTERS, RIVER RAFTING, PACK TRIPS
FLY FISHING SCHOOLS

Those out-of-staters who want to come to Montana for some good outdoor recreation and trout fishing might consider reserving three or four nights with a reputable outfitter or guest ranch. There are many of them in southern Montana, and at most of them lodging and meals are provided..

They offer a variety of options, any of which provide a good measure of excitement. The most popular draw is floating rivers and fly fishing as you go. One outfitter offers a several-day trip that includes stopping at various points and camping overnight. The equipment is provided, with training if necessary. Float trips almost always guarantee a good catch along the way.

Another option is walk-in trips, which simply means the fishing is done from the bank. This offers better conditions for training to fly fish. Some may prefer this to floating the river.

There is also the option of going into high country on horseback. This not only provides excellent fishing, but some breath taking scenery. If desired, the trip can be just for sightseeing. These pack trips are guided by professionals who are trained and are very familiar with the country. They will take along entire families, even multiple families. If you plan to go without a guide, it is highly recommended that you do not go alone.

They are equipped to handle any intrusion by bears. They know how to scare them off before they get near. Horseback is safer than hiking on foot because the horse is more sure footed when on somewhat dangerous trails. Accidents are better handled, too, in case someone should fall. If a leg is broken when far from the vehicle into difficult terrain, it is much easier to go back on horse than be carried.

Those who head for a particular place in high country for the first time, generally do not know where to fish as do outfitters. Where to fish and what to use will guarantee some good fishing. One outfitter provides pack trips into Yellowstone Park.

Below is a list of established outfitters, lodges, guest ranches and guide services. Among other things, they provide horse pack trips, fishing guide services, river rafting, white water rafting and, at most of them, lodging and meals. It is divided into three southern Montana areas: east, central, and west. In choosing a place to lodge or other activity it is suggested you pick one nearest the place you want to fish or do other recreation. At the end is a list of fly fishing schools, if you would like some schooling and training before you venture into it.

The list is, of course, subject to change, but these places are, for the most part, well established:

Southeast

Bighorn Trout Shop   (406)666 2375
    Fort Smith, MT   Located at Yellowtail Dam on the Bighorn River
    Modern comfortable rooms, fine dining
    Fly fishing on premier trout stream, guided float fishing trips

Beartrap Ranch   (406) 698 2224
    Clark's Fork Valley (60 miles south of Billings)
    Lodging and dining   Open year round
    Near premier trout stream - Big Horn River
    Short trip to famous Buffalo Bill Historical Museum
    Yellowstone Park- drive through in one day
    Family activities including stocked fishing pond for children

Cottonwood Camp   (406)666 2391
    Near Fort Smith on Big Horn River
    Cabins
    Fishing float trips on the Big Horn

Five Rivers Lodge   (800)378 5006
    Dillon, MT   Guided fishing trips

Bud Lilly Trout Shop   (406)646 7801
    West Yellowstone, MT
    Guided Fishing trips on Madison, Henry's Fork and
    Yellowstone rivers

Southcentral

Chico Hot Springs   (406) 333 4933
>
> Paradise Valley south of Livingston, MT
> Luxury resort. Main lodge or cozy cabins.   Fine Dining   Year around
> Natural hot springs pools. Horseback trips, float trips
> Fly fishing on renowned Spring Creeks
> Other family activities. Close to north entrance to Yellowstone Park

Paradise Gateway Bed and Breakfast and Guest Cabins   (800)541 4113
>
> Emigrant, MT   Near north entrance to Yellowstone Park
> Fishing on Yellowstone River, and in the park.

Big Horn Resort   (406)839 9300
>
> Billings, MT
> Luxury resort. Lodging, dining
> Horseback rides, river rafting, several tours to historical sites
> Water park: wave pool, water slides over 300'

Paintbrush Adventures   (406) 328 4158
>
> Absarokee, MT   Hiking, pack trips, fishing trips
> Fishing on Stillwater River, other streams and lakes

Blue Sky Cabins   (406) 446 0186
>
> Red Lodge, MT
> Luxury cabins at foot of mountains. Secluded.   Fishing and other activities
> One day trip through Yellowstone Park. Fishing pond for children

Rock Creek Resort   (800) 667 1119
>
> Red Lodge, MT (5 miles south)
> Luxury lodging and dining
> Fishing on Rock Creek. Easy one day trip through Yellowstone Park
> Special activities for children, including pool
> Golf course

Montana Whitewater Rafting Co   (800) 779 4465
>
> Gardiner, MT (NW entrance to Yellowstone Park)
> Fly fishing for beginners, rafting and other activities
> Yellowstone, Gallatin and Madison rivers

High Country Outfitters Fly Fishing Lodge   (406) 333 4763
    Gardiner, MT
    Lodging, dining, guided fishing trips

Stillwater Anglers   (855)785 5987
    Columbus, MT
    Fly fishing and outfitting services
    Stillwater River, Yellowstone River, Boulder River, others

Angler's West   (406) 333 4401
    Emigrant, MT
    Fly fishing Outfitters

Flying Pig Adventure Co   (866)807 0744
    Gardiner, MT
    Lodging and dining.   Outdoor dining around campfire
    Several adventure packages for families
    Horseback rides w/cookouts, horseback fishing trips, white water rafting

Long Outfitting   (406) 222 6775
    Livingston, MT
    Fishing trips on Yellowstone River. Full and half day float or wade fishing trips.

Big Moose Resort   (406)838 2303
    Cook City, MT
    Guest cabins with kitchenettes
    Short distance to northeast entrance to Yellowstone Park

Beartooth Plateau Outfitters   (800)253 8545
    Cook City, MT
    Fly fishing, horseback trips

Southwest
Madison Valley Ranch   (800)891 6151
  Ennis, MT   Lodging and dining
    Beautiful lodge, trout fishing on blue ribbon trout stream - Madison River

Big Hole Lodge   (406)832 3252
     Excellent lodging and dining
     Big Hole River minutes away.   Excellent dry fly fishing
     Also Beaverhead River and Ruby River fishing trips
     Private stream fishing, well stocked

Absaroka-Beartooth Outfitters   (406)579 3866
     Bozeman, MT
     Fly fishing. Fishing float trips. 5-day wilderness pack trip.

Lone Mountain Ranch   (800)514 4644
     Big Sky, MT
     Orvis "Fly Fishing Lodge of the Year"
     Fly fishing, pack trips, many other activities
     Yellowstone Park tours

Geyser Whitewater Expeditions   (800)914 9031
     Big Sky, Montana
     Whitwater Rafting, Zipline, Horseback riding, Bike riding

River's Edge   (March thru Early May)   (406)586 5373
     Bozeman, Montana
     Fishing float trips on Yellowstone, Madison, Gallatin, and Big Horn rivers

Montana Troutfitters Shop, Bozeman Montana   (406)587 4707
     Float trips on several streams and private lakes

Montana Trout Stalkers   (406)581 5150
     Ennis, MT
     Guided fishing trips on several rivers. Full, half day and overnight trips
     Horseback trip to a alpine lake to fish
     Fly fishing school

Galatin River Lodge   (406)388 6766
     Bozeman, MT
     Guided trips

Canyon Creek Ranch   (800)560 2688
    Melrose, MT
    Lodging, meals, fly fishing, horseback trips, river rafting
    Limited to four families at a time

FLY FISHING SCHOOLS

Brant Oswald, Fly Fishing Instructor.   (406) 587 9111
    Bozeman, MT
    (Contact Bozeman Angler)

Lyn Dawson   Fly Fishing Instructor   www,dawsonflyfishing.com
    Bozeman, MT

Montana State University   7-week course   (406) 652 8330
    Bozeman, MT

Bob Tusken's MT School of Fly Fishing   (406) 451 4475
    West Yellowstone, MT

Montana Trout Stalkers   (406)581 5150
    Ennis, MT

CHAPTER 14
PLACES TO LODGE FOR FISHING TRIPS AND OTHER RECREATIONAL ACTIVITIES

Those who come from out of state to fish in southern Montana may wonder where to find lodging from which to travel to the streams. Those who plan to hike and fish in the high mountain areas may want to consider going to a lodge, guest ranch, or outfitter that sponsors these trips. They usually provide food, lodging and everything else one needs for the trip into the mountains (see chapter 13). If you intend to spend some days touring the streams reachable by road then you will need to rent a motel in one of the towns along interstate 90 or on a connecting highway.

Billings seen from the rimrocks to the north. Yellowstone River just under cliffs

BILLINGS, MONTANA
THE COUNTRYSIDE

The countryside around Billings consists mainly of rolling prairies
with numerous picturesque sandstone cliffs. To the north, lies
the rugged Bull Mountains, which consists of high hills and deep
ravines covered with pine trees, spotted with wide open prairies and
green valleys. Whitetail deer are abundant in the area, sometimes
grazing right in the city.   Deer hunting is a big attraction in
Montana, and many hike these areas for game and usually do not
come up empty handed.

THE COUNTRYSIDE NORTHWEST OF BILLINGS
WOODED HILLS TO THE NORTH, YELLOWSTONE VALLY IN THE DISTANCE

WIDE OPEN PRARIES NEAR MUSSELSHELL RIVER NORTH OF BILLINGS

Billings

This is the largest city in Montana with an abundance of hotels and motels. Sometimes when families come to the area some go fishing while others stay behind to enjoy the recreation and shopping in the city. Billings can be a springboard to a lot of sightseeing and other recreation in the state. (See chapter 13)

From Billings, one can readily drive in less than an hour to any of several streams: the Big Horn, Clark's Fork, Rock Creek, and the Stillwater. If supplies are needed, there are some fly shops along 24th street west or the Big Bear Sports Center on King avenue. There are knowledgeable anglers in these places who can provide information on the fishing and what to use.

By driving to the top of the rimrocks north of Billings, the location of the airport, you can get a good view of the city with the majestic Beartooth and Prior Mountains in the background. Looking down at the city, you can see a multiplex of buildings nestled near the down town business district. This is the huge medical corridor which has two large hospital complexes adjacent to each other, providing extensive medical services to a large area in the northwest.

Bozeman

This small city of nearly 40,000, sits in a beautiful setting, the very green and fertile Gallatin Valley surrounded on three sides by mountain ranges. About 10 miles to the west is the Gallatin River. This town and scenic areas surrounding it, have become popular with various entertainment and other prominent people, forcing land values to increase dramatically.

It is home to Montana State University and has attracted many sports minded people, whether it be fishing and hunting or skiing at one of two popular ski resorts nearby. This is an excellent location from which to make a short drive to good trout streams: Yellowstone River (30 miles east), Gallatin River (10 miles west) and the Madison River (50 miles west), another of the blue ribbon trout streams in the country.

There are plenty of fine motels and restaurants. About 80 miles to the south through Gallatin Valley, is the west entrance to Yellowstone Park.

West Yellowstone

This small tourist town, on the west entrance to Yellowstone Park, is full of shops featuring all kinds of western art and jewelry. Many western artists have their works on display and for sale. For many years, a custom jeweler there has had a shop that displays some very original and beautiful rings and other jewelry.

It has many motels, but it is important to reserve rooms early because the town fills up fast during tourist season. For things to do in the evening, there is a very entertaining amateur play theater staffed by college students working there for the summer. Also, you would not want to miss the Grizzly and Wolf Discovery Center that has interesting exhibits, including live bears and wolves   It also has the IMAX Theater with a three story high screen and digital quality surround sound
.

From this town, you can travel to fish in the upper waters of the Gallatin or the Madison Rivers. There is also good fishing in three lakes nearby: Hebgen Lake, Quake Lake, and Henry's Lake.

Three Forks and Manhattan

Three rivers come together here to form the Missouri River: the Gallatin, Madison, and Jefferson Rivers. This is where the well-known Bud Lilly lived his early years, and has been active for many decades, working to preserve good trout fishing. These three rivers, and the upper Missouri, are readily accessible from these towns.

Livingston and Gardiner

Livingston is a community of about 7,500 that sits on the Yellowstone river where it comes from Yellowstone Park to the South and bends to the East. It has numerous quality motels and is basically in the center of southern Montana. Trout fishing is very popular and is somewhat of a highlight in the area. The Park is an hour drive to the south. Gardiner is a small tourist town by the Park entrance that is full of western and Native American shops. Good fishing is readily accessible on the Yellowstone River and the Boulder River is just a short hop to the east from Livingston.

Columbus and Absarokee

The Stillwater River enters the Yellowstone River at this location, and 15 miles south, the Rosebud River enters the Stillwater River. All three are good trout streams. South of Columbus is the small town of Absarokee, from where there is quick access to nice campgrounds on the Stillwater and Rosebud rivers. This whole area has some very scenic roads on which one can do some enjoyable sightseeing. The Woodbine Falls and Woodbine Cascade at the headwaters of the Stillwater River are something to see!

Big Timber

Near this town is where the Boulder River runs into the Yellowstone. The Boulder River is one of many excellent trout streams; and it, too, has some beautiful scenery around it, including the Natural Bridge Falls. At the headwaters of the Main Boulder River, well into the mountains, are some nice campgrounds; and the river gets very picturesque due to some very large boulders in the river.

The small community of McCloud is about 25 miles south of Big Timber where the West fork of the Boulder flows into the Main Boulder. The community has some cabins for rent that would be convenient for fishermen planning to stay in the area for a while.

Red Lodge

This community is a well known tourist town and also serves as a ski resort. It is a quaint little town that sits on highway 212. Further south, this road makes many hairpin turns as it approaches the majestic Beartooth Pass, at over 11,000 feet. The scenery is breathtaking! A well known news commentator for one of the major networks, said it is the most beautiful drive in the United States. Southwest another 30 miles, is the northeast entrance to Yellowstone Park.

A pretty mountain stream, Rock Creek, runs through town and provides some good fishing for small rainbow trout. Tourists also enjoy the numerous western and Indian shops here.

Cook City and Silver Gate

This is a small mountain tourist town near the northeast entrance to Yellowstone Park. It has some interesting history in that it began as a gold mining town in the late 1800s, hosting, at one time, upwards of 1000 prospectors. Billings residents like to make a day of it, driving to the town. On the way, they pass through Red Lodge and then just south go up switchbacks on the way to Beartooth pass. In town they enjoy eating a delicious meal in one of the many family restaurants. They can take in the several western shops or even do a little trout fishing on the Clark' Fork River before making the three-hour drive home. Or they stay the night in one of the fine motels and lodges..

Dillon and Twin Bridges

These are two small cities in the southwestern part of the state in which one can find nice lodging while trout fishing the area. There are several trout streams nearby, all of which are discussed in chapter one.

Ennis

The small tourist town of Ennis lies about 40 miles southwest of Bozeman. It is a good place to find accommodations while fishing one of the best trout streams in the West, the Madison River. With a western theme, it has numerous gift shops and other quaint stores. It is in a beautiful setting, sitting on the river in the beautiful Madison Valley and surrounded by three mountain ranges; The Madison Range, the Gravelly Range and the Tobacco Root Mountains.

Virgina City and Nevada City

About 30 miles west of Ennis are the old gold mining towns of Virginia City and Nevada City. You will see preserved what were once wild west boom towns, having lots of the original old historical buildings and other artifacts. Lodging can be had in some old restored hotels. Nevada City has more than a 100 buildings, including museums, restaurants, gift shops, music halls, hotels, cabins and train rides.

CHAPTER 15
OTHER FAMILY ACTIVITIES AVAILABLE

Families coming to Montana to trout fish may also want to consider other recreational activities available in the area. The following is a partial list of these activities:

Horseback trips into the mountains for sightseeing, fishing, camping
(See chapter 13)

Float trips for sightseeing or fishing available on several rivers
(See chapter 13)

Exciting white water float trips
Excellent for a adrenalin rush.
Extra precautions taken for safety.
Well qualified guides attend each raft.
(See chapter 13)

Hunting
Southern Montana deer and elk hunting attracts hundreds of hunters from out of state every year. There are numerous professional guides who can take hunting parties into areas with a good population of game. Bow hunting has become very popular and the season for bows starts before guns   Hunting starts in October and extends into December.

Chico Hot Springs south of Livingston

This is a very popular family getaway for Billings residents. It has a variety of excellent family activities to keep the parents and kids entertained.

Yellowstone Park

This is one of the most beautiful and unique parks in North America. Yellowstone Falls is absolutely breathtaking. The numerous geysers and other thermal sights are very colorful, unseen elsewhere in the country. The Old Faithful Geyser has a rare characteristic in that it spouts off at regular intervals about 50 minutes apart.

A family can make the tour through it in one day, traveling from Billings or one of the other towns along Interstate 90. Lodging can be reserved in the park at any of several locations, but this should be done early in the year. Other possible places to stay over night are West Yellowstone at the west entrance or Cook City near the northeast entrance.

Buffalo Bill Historical Museum

This is an outstanding museum located in Cody, Wyoming, just 100 miles south of Billings.   It has very extensive exhibits of western art and sculpture by famous artists and Indian displays depicting just about everything concerning their culture At times, they have had huge gun collections on display that go back centuries.

The town of Cody sits on the highway going to the east entrance to Yellowstone Park.   It has numerous western and Indian shops and some interesting historical places to see.

Beartooth Scenic Highway

This is a three hour drive from Red Lodge, 60 miles southwest of Billings, to Cook City at the northeast entrance to Yellowstone Park. The summit, Beartooth Pass, which is on the Montana/Wyoming border is over 11,000 feet providing sky top views of snow capped peaks, glaciers, alpine lakes and plateaus. There are numerous switchbacks on both sides of the summit. It is considered by some as the most beautiful drive in the United States. When arriving at Cook City, you can stop at one of the many family restaurants for some good home cooking.

Lewis and Clark Caverns

This is one of the largest caverns in the United States, having regular guided tours through it. It is a limestone labyrinth with natural rooms and hallways and exotic colorful formations with strange shapes created by slow dripping of limestone water. Big eared bats inhabit some areas.

Virginia City

This is a preserved gold and ruby mining town with many of the old buildings still being maintained. There are numerous exhibits of old hotels, saloons, and interesting shops. It is located 30 miles west of the town of Ennis, which sits on the Madison river, and about 80 miles west of Bozeman. For recreation, you can pan for gold or rubies in creeks nearby.

The Badlands

An extensive area of desolate land, yet unique with some breathtaking scenery, in eastern Montana. There are areas where there is on-going digging for dinosaur fossils, such as the Makoshika State Park near the town of Terry. At the entrance, there is a dinosaur museum and visitor center. Another such museum is located in the town of Glendive, to the northeast.

Dinolab

At this facility in Billings, paleontologists process dinosaur bones recovered from different areas in the Badlands and elsewhere. Visitors can observe the work being done. The bones are cased in plaster before they are removed from the soil, and then at the center, removed from the plaster, cleaned and prepared for display.

Little Bighorn Battlefield National Monument

In 1876, this is where the U.S. 7th Cavalry was crushed by Lakota Sioux, Cheyenne, and Arapaho warriors at the battle of the Little Bighorn. There were 263 soldiers killed, including Lt. Col. George Armstrong Custer. It is

VIRGINIA CITY AND NEVADA CITY

OLD HOME & PICKUP

LOOKS LIKE HOUSE OF SEVEN GABLES

OLD WAGON WHEEL

OLD SHOPS

AND BUILDINGS

PRESERVED

referred to as the Custer Battlefield. This monument, about 60 miles west of Billings, has tours of the battlefield and a museum. There is also an yearly reenactment of this battle staged during the month of June.

For more information and to visit the Big Horn County Historical Museum and the Little Bighorn National Monument contact the Hardin Chamber of Commerce - (406)665-1672

Rosebud Battlefield State Park
This is a memorial of one of the greatest battles between the Indian and the white man, involving a force of about 1300 on each side.   Just prior to the battle of the Little Bighorn where General Custer and his men were wiped out, this battle took place on the Rosebud River, a short distance to the west.

Big Horn Canyon recreation area
About 50 miles east of Billings, is this long deep canyon with incredible walls in some places exceeding 1000 feet above the Big Horn Lake, enjoyed for its stillness and quite.   It is a big attraction for those who love boating, and there are numerous campgrounds that can be reached only by boat.   The lake contains trout, bass, walleye and other fish.

Zoo Montana
Many of the native Rocky Mountain wild animals can be seen here along with other animals such as lions and tigers. It is located just west of Billings.

Alberta Bair Theater
Located in downtown Billings, this quality theater has an ongoing variety of excellent live entertainment.

Montana Avenue, Billings
Many of the old buildings on this street in downtown Billings have been restored and are occupied by quaint cafes, shops and art vendors.

Lake Elmo
This small lake is in the northeast section of Billings. It is stocked with rainbow trout and other fish. Many persons enjoy just relaxing on the shore with a refreshing drink and still fishing from shore using worms or other bait.

There is a small beach for families with children to enjoy swimming, which is actually allowed in all of the lake. One of the headquarters of the Montana Fish, Wildlife and Parks is located on the south side of the lake and is open to the public to get fishing information about the south central part of the state.

West Yellowstone
See chapter 14

Ski Resorts
Southern Montana has three well known ski resorts: Red Lodge, Bridger Bowl at Bozeman, and Big Sky. These ski runs provide excellent skiing in the winter months, but there are other entertainment activities throughout the year.

Zipline Adventure
See the comments in Big Sky Resort below.

Ziplining
High
Above
Ground

Big Sky Resort

Soar through the pine trees and gullies, high above the ski trails. Such is the zipline adventure offered by Geyser Whitewater Expeditions at Big Sky Resort, located on highway 191 south of Bozeman. Whereas white water rafting is the main recreation offered by them, they have this to say in their brochure, "Pair your raft trip with a horseback ride , zipline adventure, guided bike ride, or boat rentals at the Marina at Lake Levinsky for an unforgettable day of family fun.......and have lunch at the Broken Oar Cafe.

Big Sky Resort at Night

MONTANA - "YOU GOTTA SEE IT"

This publication has given you somewhat of a picture of what Montana is like. Words do not do it justice. You have to see and experience it. I have encountered numerous families who are making it a practice to yearly come to the state to enjoy the many outdoor activities. While trout fishing is perhaps the biggest draw, many are also coming to experience white water rafting, horse pack trips into the high mountains, and many other outdoor activities, including going to see the many western historical and cultural sights.

The whole state of Montana has much to offer. (See the quote by Governor Switzer at the beginning of the book) It is a state of very diverse landscapes, from high mountains to beautiful green valleys and wide open prairies. The whole western side of the state is one long stretch of mountains with numerous trout streams. The central part is mostly prairie, farm and ranch land, with a few small mountain ranges. The eastern part of the state has an area that is at the other end of the spectrum, known as the "Bad Lands". Even the rattlesnakes are said to curse it. However, it has a unique beauty to it.

The northwestern part of the state has the majestic Glacier National Park, and one of the largest freshwater lakes in the country, Flathead Lake. The central and eastern part of the state has the Charles M. Russell Wildlife Refuge, encompassing the 100 mile long Fort Peck Lake. Fishermen come to this lake in pursuit of a variety of fish: kokanee salmon, lake trout, smallmouth bass, yellow perch, norther pike, sauger, sturgeon and walleye pike. When you hook into a fish, you don't know what you have got until you land it.

There are also a number of Indian reservations in the state that add a lot of color to the state's culture. At various times, there are Indian powwows around the state, that can be very entertaining to watch as they dance in their native dress.

Part of the journey of the famous Lewis and Clark expedition cats across Montana. In 1806, in a place east of Billings called Pompey's Pillar, Captain William Clark and his party left their mark. Lewis had taken a different route, and they were to join up later. Clark, along with his guide, Sacagawea, and her infant son stopped at this location as they were traveling by canoe on the Yellowstone River. Clark had nicknamed the son "Pomp" or "Little Pomp," from which the name Pompey's Pillar came about.

APPENDIX

TROUT UNLIMITED (TU)

This is a national organization dedicated to the conservation and preservation of trout. Nationwide there are 140,000 members in 400 chapters in the United States and Canada, and the headquarters is in Arlington, Virginia. Once chapter in Billings Montana is the Magic City Fly Fishers (MCFF), number 582.

The MCFF works closely with various organizations, government agencies, and other entities to preserve, conserve and restore fish habitat in southcentral Montana. Other activities included are:

■ Lessons in fly typing, casting, rod building and other fly fishing activities.
■ Serves as a regional advocate for maintaining adequate flows on the Big Horn River.
■ Actively involved in projects to preserve and restore native Yellowstone trout in the upper Yellowstone River drainage.
■ Other activities to bring trout fishermen together for social interaction.

Montana has 13 chapters with 3,400 members. To learn more or if interested in becoming a member in the Billings area, log onto www.mcffonline.org or info@mcffonline.org. If interested in contacting a different chapter, simply go to Trout Unlimited on the internet.

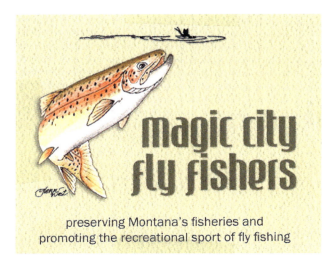

THE SPECIES OF TROUT
ON DISPLAY AT THE TROUT UNLIMITED FACILITY IN WEST YELLOWSTONE
(FACILITY HAS MOVED TO DIFFERENT LOCATION)

BROOK   GRAYLING   BROWN

RAINBOW   CUTTHROAT

BUD LILLY, WELL KNOWN TROUT PRESERVATIONIST

This man is well known among trout enthusiasts around the country. He was the first president of Montana Trout Unlimited, founder of the Montana Trout Foundation and first chairman of the International Fly Fishing Center. He has authored several books, including the *Handbook for Western Trout Fishing* which has been a favorite of trout fishermen.

It is a fact that the trout streams and trout fishing have been under attack by various activities such as developing, streamside home building, well digging, and sewage that finds its way into the streams. It has been the objective of TU, Bud Lilly and others to counter much of this activity to protect the clear water of the streams and rivers and the fishing. To some extent, it has paid off, due to the hard efforts of numerous volunteers.

He grew up in Manhattan, in southwest Montana near the town of Three Forks, which derives its name from the fact that three rivers come together here to form the Missouri River. These rivers are the Madison, Jefferson, and Gallatin, all of which have good trout fishing. Lilly has operated a fly fishing store in Three Forks for many years.

ENCOUNTERING BEARS AND MOOSE

There are certain dangers involved when fishing or backpacking in the mountains. If a black bear or grizzly should be encountered, there is usually not much of a threat unless it is a sow with cubs. If a sow with cubs is encountered, it is important to keep your eyes on the bear and slowly back away and leave the area. Bears can run fast, even outrun a horse in 50 yards. A park ranger reported that they can cover 100 yards in seven seconds. A preventative measure is to wear a small bell on your jacket. The ringing will usually scare the bear off long before you run into him

If a bear charges, get into your car right away. If you are no where near the car, then you are in serious trouble. In anticipation of this, it is good to have pepper spray, or bear spray, wait until it is within a few feet, and then shoot for the face. This will usually repel the bear. Some carry a pistol, but it needs to be higher than a 32 caliber to drop the bear. If it makes contact, try to hit it on the nose with a stick or your fist. As a last resort, if the bear has you down, get into a fetal position to protect vital organs and do your best to act dead, even when it may be biting. Do not stand directly in front of a standing bear because it can kill with one swipe of its huge paw. It is a fact that a very large grizzly has killed a horse with one swipe. There is a lot of information about what to do when attacked by a bear which is discussed in numerous outdoor type books,

A moose can also be dangerous. A man who does a lot of backpacking said he and a friend had to run from a bull moose, and finally climb a tree to safety. The bull kept them there all night. If the moose overcomes you, it will stomp on you which, due to its size, can be fatal. If you suddenly run into one, walk very slowly and leave the area, and it probably will not attack. If it is a sow with a calf, this too can be especially dangerous because she may attack to protect her calf. One thing to do when being chased by a moose, is to get a large tree between you and the moose.

When embarking on a backpacking trip, check the sign at the head of the trail that explains the danger of bears and certain things to avoid that may attract them. One example is to hang your food from a tree away from your tent. There are also certain cautions about perfume and other cosmetics.

This information is not to scare anyone away from hiking or fishing in the mountains. These encounters are pretty rare, but it is the course of wisdom to prepare for any possible situation.

BLUE RIBBON

TROPHIES

BIG HORN

BEAUTIES

BIG HORN LUNKERS

144

THE MUSSELSHELL RIVER

SMALL STREAM BIG FISH

MADISON TROPHIES

GOT THE BRAGGIN RIGHTS

FOR THE YEAR

YA
WE GET'EM
IN THE
WINTER
TOO

NOT
TOO
SHABBY

GOT
REASON
TO SMILE

Made in the USA
Monee, IL
11 December 2024